THE NORTH SEA EARLS

THE NORTH SEA EARLS

The Shetland/Viking Archaeological Expedition

Ian Morrison

GENTRY BOOKS · LONDON

First published 1973

ISBN 0 85614 028 7

Published by GENTRY BOOKS LIMITED,
15, Tooks Court, London, EC4A 1LA
Layout and design Brian Roll
Printed by Lowe & Brydone (Printers) Ltd.
London, Thetford and Haverhill.

Contents

For A.N.M. and A.K.M.

Illustrations

PHOTOGRAPHIC ILLUSTRATIONS

MAPS

LINE DRAWINGS

Editorial Note

The results that the Shetland Viking Expedition achieved reflect the efforts of almost a hundred people. This book was written in recognition of this, and in gratitude for the sponsorship of Gentry Books Ltd. It was produced and illustrated by Ian Morrison, with the approval of Alan Bax and Jim Gill on behalf of the Expedition.

The Expedition was engaged in various kinds of academic detective work, but this is not a formal 'academic' book. Some of the papers in scholarly journals discussing aspects of the Expedition's findings are noted at the end of the book. Others are in preparation. For the Expedition, Dr. Lucy Collings reviewed and revised passages of the late Dr. A.B. Taylor's translations of *Orkneyinga Saga.* Since specialists may consult her technical work elsewhere (in *Collings, Farrell* and *Morrison:* see book list) it appeared more appropriate to use a less literal approach here and in the interests of readability the Saga extracts are therefore very free paraphrases, though the aim has been to keep these compatible with the accepted readings of Drs. Taylor and Collings. Some of the maps use unconventional viewpoints and projections to illustrate Shetland's position. These were prepared using facilities of the Geography Department at Edinburgh University.

Preface

The Earls who give this book its title were Norsemen. *Orkneyinga Saga* tells how their Viking longships were wrecked in the Shetland Islands north of Scotland, in the middle of the twelfth century. The book is not an academic treatise on them, but an informal account of detective work carried out in Shetland by an expedition made up of amateur divers with some professional leadership. They looked into the circumstances of the wrecking, and followed one of the Earls, Rognvald, to Sumburgh at the southern tip of the islands, where the Viking settlement of Jarlshof stands as one of the most remarkable archaeological sites of the British Isles. There, soon after the wreck, Rognvald again found himself in peril on the sea.

The Expedition leaders included Lt. Cdr. Alan Bax of the Fort Bovisand Underwater Centre, Plymouth, who ran the diving operations with his partners, Messrs. Jim Gill and Nic Ashmore. Prof. Robert Farrell looked after administration and project coordination, as well as investigating linguistic points with Dr. Lucy Collings, a colleague of his at Cornell. Dr. Ian Morrison of Edinburgh University was in charge of geographical and archaeological research into Shetland landscapes and seascapes of the time of the Earls.

The Expedition was an international one, with American as well as British members. Even those from Britain, from south of the Pentland Firth, found much that was strange to them in the everyday life of the islands. In Shetland more than in any other part of the United Kingdom Norse elements live on, partly surviving from the Viking age and partly enlivened by continuing contacts with Scandinavia.

This then is the story of an expedition in pursuit of the wrecked Viking Earls: what the divers sought along the cliffs and on the sea-bed; what they found out about *Orkneyinga Saga*; and what caught their imagination about the Norse legacy of present day Shetland.

Chapter 1

The Expedition

Crash we went, with *Hjolp* and *Fifa*
  – both were wrecked;
The seasprays brought them sorrow,
The waves gave grief to men.
I see this voyage of the Earls
  – will be remembered - - -
  said Rognvald

On a dark Thursday night in the year 1148 A.D., the crews of two Viking ships suddenly sensed breakers all round them in the gloom. They had been caught in a storm after leaving Norway two days before, and now they were unsure of their position. But the surf told them that they were embayed, and they had no choice but to run both ships ashore while they still maintained at least a measure of control of the situation. The men survived but the vessels were completely wrecked, and they lost many of their goods. These were no ordinary losses, for both the ships and their cargoes were special gifts, aimed at cementing an alliance between young King Ingi of

Norway and Rognvald, the powerful Viking Earl of the Northern Isles of Scotland.

As a parting gift when Rognvald decided to return from Bergen to his base in Orkney, Ingi presented him with *Hjolp* and *Fifa* ("Help" and "Arrow"). *Orkneyinga Saga* describes them as being very beautiful, and claims that "of all ships they were the swiftest". The King's advisors foresaw trouble in Norway, so along with the longships he showered "great gifts" on his potential ally. The Saga tells us that the Earl also received "many other great gifts" from his own kinsmen and friends in that country. From the practice of the period, we may guess that these included such things as decorated weapons, fine clothes, jewellery, furs, and so forth.

Rognvald himself sailed in *Hjolp.* He gave *Fifa* over to the young Earl Harald, who was then only fourteen or fifteen years old. The boy had asked particularly to be allowed to accompany him to Bergen for the experience of a trip overseas. He had perhaps taken on rather more than he had expected.

As they struggled clear of the surf, they decided that the storm must have carried them north of their proper course for Orkney, and concluded that they had probably been cast away on Shetland. They were right. Despite mist and darkness they soon found farmsteads and roused out the Norse crofters. Large fires were made for them, and they tried to get the chill of the autumn sea out of their bones. A local girl called Asa went out of the house where Rognvald had been taken in, to get water for the survivors. In the fog she missed her footing and fell into the well. She came in, soaked through and shivering so hard that nobody could follow what she was saying. Rognvald was by then in good spirits, but he knew only too well how she felt, after his own recent plunge. Indeed he claimed that he could interpret her despite her chattering teeth:—

"You sit cosy at the fire,
  While Asa – atatata –
  Lies in water – hutututu –
Where shall I sit? I am frozen . . . "

With details like these, the Saga conjures up a most vivid picture of the events of that night. We shall look at this more closely in later chapters.

It is noticeable that in viewing the past, major but long-term developments often fail to catch the imagination in quite the way that minor events may. Although we can accept the verdicts of the

'Asa'

professional historians as to the importance of slow economic or social changes, it is difficult to feel any real involvement with them. With incidents like the shipwreck of the Earls on the other hand, we find ourselves identifying directly with the participants and imagining that we can grasp something of their experience on that night. If you have ever yourself been lost in a small boat in low visibility, and suddenly heard breakers . . . or, more mundanely, even if you simply remember getting soaked at a bus stop, and coming home with your teeth chattering, then you feel some human contact with Rognvald and Asa. This feeling may be anathema to some concerned with the pursuit of "historical objectivity", but it is undeniably exciting.

The Shetland Viking Expedition grew out of excitement of this kind, generated by the Saga. Three of the leaders, Alan Bax, Jim Gill and Ian Morrison had been in the Shetlands previously, working on the wreck of a Dutch East Indiaman called *Liefde* that was lost in the Out Skerries in 1711. They are a far-travelled trio but they were agreed that Shetland was one of the most intriguing places they had ever come across, and that they would like to return there if a worthwhile project presented itself. It was clear that the chances of actually finding material from the longships was slim indeed, but there was another aspect to the wrecking of the Earls that offered the prospect of bringing together "the excitement" with "the quest for historical objectivity".

It arose out of the basic nature of the Saga. In it, details like the anecdote about Asa's chattering teeth bring the account of Rognvald to life in a most persuasive way. The section on the wrecking contains several other little stories all very obviously told in order to illustrate how in that time of stress "Earl Rognvald, as ever, bore himself the best of all men . . . " The writer of *Orkneyinga Saga*, like many of the other writers of family or history sagas, was clearly anything but naive in his manipulation of telling detail to produce vivid portrayals of the people of interest to him. Like those writers too, his aim was not so much to attempt an "objective history" as to blend historical fact and plausible characterisation to produce an aesthetically satisfying and perhaps politically useful model of behaviour. Whether Rognvald was in real life quite the man the Saga makes him out to be is thus perhaps a moot point. Furthermore, some of the incidents used to "sell the image" of the Earl may themselves be apocryphal. Did Rognvald really show he was unperturbed amid catastrophe by immediately composing verses, like the one at the head of this chapter and one about Asa? In fact, did the Asa incident actually happen? Or was it introduced by the saga writer for effect? Indeed, did the shipwrecks occur as described, or was the whole incident manipulated beyond recognition to provide a showcase for the points that the writer wished to emphasise about the Earl's character?

In many of the sagas, historical fact and historical fiction are almost inextricably mingled. Scholars are thus always on the lookout for new ways of testing the historical veracity of different passages. In many cases, the events described are not of types susceptible to empirical investigation. Bob Farrell, who works on early literature, suggested that the description of the wrecking of Earls Rognvald and Harald might offer grounds for a test. As we shall see in later chapters, it contains certain circumstantial details that the Expedition could check out through detective work with air photographs, echo-sounders and, above all, divers.

It was decided in the early planning stages that it was likely that an expedition would at least be able to establish whether or not the Saga account of the wrecking made sense in terms of the part of Shetland's coastline to which it was attributed. The chance of clinching matters by actually locating artefacts from the wrecks on the sea-bed was regarded as a very attractive but rather unlikely bonus. The hulls of the ships themselves seem to have been

A corner of Lerwick harbour

A traditional croft house, restored as a folk museum. Compare with the Viking houses of Jarlshof illustrated in Chapter 6

thoroughly smashed up during the night of the wreck itself. The only possibility was thus to look for small objects that might have rolled into the protection of cracks in the rocks. If they had survived at all after eight centuries of immersion, they would probably be disguised in heavy carapaces of concretion. Finds are made quite often of such objects in underwater archaeological work, but generally only after the site of a wreck has been pin-pointed by some lucky discovery. In this case, the divers could not hope to have their attention drawn to the right area by stumbling across anything as large and characteristic as a pile of cannons on the seabed. *Hjolp* and *Fifa* were half a millennium too early for that. Clearly, underwater prospecting apparatus, effective seabed survey methods, and a large team of disciplined divers would be required.

Even this level of effort seemed worth undertaking if there was the slimmest chance of making a find, however. The justly famous Viking ship finds in Scandinavia, whether in burial mounds or on the seabed, are all of nameless vessels without a specific history. To find traces of known ships directly associated with figures like Earls Rognvald and Harald from *Orkneyinga Saga* would be unique. Furthermore, the period of the wrecks was one of high artistic development in Scandinavia and the "great gifts" given to Rognvald would almost certainly be of considerable aesthetic as well as historic interest. Even if the search eventually proved archaeologically unproductive, the problems of mounting a major effort of this nature would certainly be useful in terms of experience with techniques of underwater search and survey.

Shetland and the Saga together offered another objective for the Expedition. According to the Saga, after the shipwreck the Earls stayed on in Shetland for some time before returning to Orkney. At one point, Rognvald visited a Norse settlement at the southern tip of the islands, and very nearly came to grief again. He pitted himself against the great tide-race off Sumburgh Head, at the oars of a local fisherman's boat. The village that he visited may have been what is now known as Jarlshof. This is one of the most exciting Viking sites to have been excavated in the United Kingdom. The archaeological reports concentrate, however, on the internal features of the settlement, rather than on its geographical setting. The site has been partly eroded by the sea, and Ian Morrison in particular was keen to try to find out what it had been like in Earl Rognvald's time: to set Jarlshof, in other words, in its Viking seascape, and investigate the rather intriguing way that the Norse seafarers had exploited their environment there.

What with the check on Saga historicity, plus the search for actual remains from the wrecks (with the prospecting and survey experiments involved in this), and then the Jarlshof project, there seemed no shortage of interesting objectives for an expedition. Neither was there a shortage of personnel.

There were over three hundred applications for a hundred places on the Expedition, despite the fact that it was made very clear that all who came would have to pay their own transport and contribute towards food and accommodation. It was emphasised too that this was no "get rich quick" hunt for sunken treasure. The basic aim was information, not gold, and it was stipulated that if any finds were made these would be turned over immediately to the Shetland museum.

The expedition ran for eight weeks in July and August of 1972. Some ten key volunteers stayed for the whole season, providing continuity in the various vital functions of the operation. Besides the leaders, these included David Shaw, Richard Price, Denis Gauci, and Pamela Butler. David and Richard were central to the diving operations. They were Englishmen, students of physics and law respectively. Denis was originally from Malta, but is not unknown at the University of Bradford. He ran the compressors that supplied the divers' air. Pam is a peripatetic potter. An American, she not only cooked for up to fifty hungry people at a sitting, but contrived to find time to learn to dive herself. Then there was one Denis Mott from Otley. Officially he came to operate electronic prospecting equipment lent by the Bradford Post Graduate School of Studies in Physics. Unofficially, he soon became known as the infallible fettler of virtually any recalcitrant piece of machinery. On a long and active expedition, sooner or later most things from pumps, water-heaters and air compressors to echosounders, proton magnetometers and Landrover cylinder-head gaskets came his way. Earl Rognvald was clearly not the only one positively to enjoy sorting out catastrophes on the shores of Shetland.

The rest of the personnel typically came in groups for a two or three week stay, often bringing their own vehicles and inflatable boats. On average, there would be about thirty underwater workers with a support team of about fifteen non-divers present in Shetland at any one time. Through the kindness of the islanders, they were able to live in the Dunrossness and then Gulberwick Parish Halls, sleeping in serried ranks on air mattresses and camp beds. There were cooking facilities, and wash-hand basins in plenty. Full scale baths, to sluice off the salt after a day's diving, provided a problem. The showers of the Seamen's Mission in Lerwick were well patronised, but extraordinary contortions were to be witnessed in the back yards of the halls as the hardier souls attempted first to insert themselves into, and then (more difficult!) extricate themselves from plastic dustbins full of suds.

The enthusiasm and sheer durability of the divers was impressive. They were all amateurs, and from an extraordinary spectrum of occupations. Yet they often did two or three dives per day, spending from four to five hours immersed in 12°C water. The main groups came from the Slough Sub-Aqua Club, the Newcastle-upon-Tyne branch of the British Sub-Aqua Club, Bradford, Brunel and Manchester Universities, and the Sub-Aqua Association of the British Army. Individual expedition members came from even further afield.

The gathering and selection of these divers was handled by Alan Bax and Jim Gill at the Fort Bovisand Underwater Centre, Plymouth. They are the leading directors, and indeed creators, of that centre, and although it stands almost as far away from Shetland as one can get and still be in Britain, the Fort was in many respects the home of the Expedition. Much of the planning and training was done there, and both equipment and expertise were drawn from its resources. Besides Alan and Jim, Nic Ashmore and Martin Black from the staff there had major roles in Shetland.

The Bovisand Underwater Centre was the home of the Expedition in a sense beyond the immediate practical one. Many people take up diving simply out of curiosity, or because they believe it will be exciting. In Britain and America, there are well organised clubs in which amateurs can learn the techniques safely and efficiently. The training in itself is interesting, but once proficiency has been gained, the diver often finds that he has acquired a technical skill and a quantity of expensive equipment, without having any real outlet for applying them. Some find satisfaction in teaching the next crop of beginners in the clubs; others become bored and drop out; a few get involved in physically (or legally) foolhardy escapades "for kicks". But with somewhere between ten and twenty thousand amateur divers in the United Kingdom, that leaves a large number who are equipped, proficient and keen to take part in any constructive enterprise.

It was in recognition of this that the Underwater Centre was set up. One can learn to dive there, *ab initio*, but many of the courses are aimed at those who already have the basic skills and wish to train in aspects of operational diving that range from underwater photography to the use of thermic lances and explosives on the seabed. With its own accommodation, workshops and harbour, Bovisand has become the diving base for a variety of academic and experimental teams. *Glaucus,* an underwater house, is located there, and miniature submarines are to be seen being built or given their sea trials.

Amid all this diverse activity, courses in underwater archaeology provide a major focus at the Fort. The notion of finding ancient wrecks and sunken cities is one that fascinates amateur divers all over the world. What divers have done to much of what they have found very often appals professional archaeologists, however. Sites that could have yielded unique and vivid glimpses of the seafarers and coastal dwellers of the past, their ships and way of life, have been destroyed by activities ranging from thoughtless souvenir hunting to calculated commercial looting. Often not only the information that the sites might have yielded through proper investigation has been lost, but even the salvaged artefacts have gone, mouldering away for want of museum laboratory conservation. In Britain, the Committee (now Council) for Nautical Archaeology was set up to attempt to do something about the situation. Alan Bax participates in this body, and the practical courses at the Fort in underwater archaeological survey and recording techniques help to channel amateur enthusiasm in constructive directions.

The groundwork laid at the Fort helped to ensure that the groups participating in the Expedition had a realistic idea of what they would be up against. There would be no dragon figureheads sticking up through the kelp jungle, to lead the way to untold riches. Instead, there would be hours of probing cracks in rocks; looking for lumps of stone that seemed geologically anomalous; meticulously plotting the positions of finds of modern junk, to find out just how objects of different kinds were moving around the most promising areas of seabed; raising boulders with compressed air; searching sand with a metal detector and a species of underwater vacuum cleaner; measuring, recording; writing up, then trying to repair the wear-and-tear on one's tattered wet-suit, so that tomorrow the hours in the water might not seem quite as numbing.

The backgrounds of the four Expedition leaders were varied, but they certainly had no romantic illusions as to what would be entailed. Alan Bax learned his diving in the Royal Navy. He joined as a boy, and rose to have his own command, before retiring early to start the Fort Bovisand Centre. His partner, Jim Gill, is an Anglo-American, who qualified as a engineer-architect at Princeton, before becoming an executive for an international oil company. He now spends part of his time applying his original training to completing the conversion of the Fort. Underwater, he specialises in photography and instructs in submarine engineering techniques. Bob Farrell teaches in the English Department at Cornell, but also works in England from time to time. Besides looking after administration in Shetland, he was often in the water. There can hardly be many studying Old Norse and Anglo-Saxon who also dive. Ian Morrison investigates the environments of ancient settlements, particularly in cases where sea level changes are involved. He has been using diving techniques in his research for about ten years now, working in the Aegean and Canaries as well as in the Scottish waters. He lectures in the Geography Department of Edinburgh University.

Although Ian Morrison is a Scot, with connections ramifying over the face of his homeland from the Hebrides to Fife and from Aberdeen to Glasgow, this gave him very little advantage over those on the Expedition who spoke with the tongues of Slough, Chicago, Otley, New York or Tyneside when it came to conversing with the Shetlanders. The islanders immediately labelled him as a "Sooth-Moother", and put him in the same class as all those other foreigners who sail into Lerwick harbour via the south entrance. To Shetlanders, "The Mainland" is unambiguously the Mainland of *Shetland*. They talk of "going to Scotland", a place quite distinct from their isles in Shetland eyes.

This was one of the chief attractions in mounting the Expedition. It gave an opportunity to live and work for a while in a part of Britain with a unique and lively culture, where a Norse element rooted in the Viking age still pervades everyday turns of speech, place-names, house and boat types, even knitting patterns and fiddle tunes.

Let us therefore set the stage for the Expedition by exploring this special Shetland setting. It constantly reminded the team that though the Earls they were pursing might be long dead, some things rooted in their era are still very much alive.

Chapter 2

Shetland Today – and the Scandinavian Legacy

FORTØING FORBUDT HER
KAIPLASS KUN FOR
LOKALE FISKEBÅTER

If you sail into the harbour of Lerwick the capital of Shetland and try to tie up at the fish market wharf, this notice warns you off. Its equivalent is there in English too ("No berthing at Market – White Fish Boats only"), but for a moment one might wonder whether one's navigation was a bit adrift, particularly since some of the fishermen on the quay are quite likely to be Norwegians or Danes speaking their own languages, and Scandinavian boats will be well to the fore in the harbour. Even aboard a Lerwick registered boat, one may well find the Shetland skipper listening to the weather forecast in Norwegian, and in general the islanders are rather more familiar with Scandinavia, Scandinavians and their languages than most other inhabitants of the United Kingdom tend to be. This shows up in some unexpected and rather delightful ways. For example, their county library has a fine shelf of Simenon's 'Maigret' stories, well read by the burghers of Lerwick. The whole shelf-ful is not in English or in French, but in Norwegian.

The Scandinavian interaction with Shetland is rooted in the Viking age, but it is certainly not a dead archaeological fact. The link has persisted through history and is very evident today. We literally do not have to look very far in order to see why. Through Norwegian eyes, Shetland is the nearest land in the North Sea to Norway. By sea, the journey from Bergen to Lerwick is shorter even than the journey from Bergen to Oslo. Aberdeen is the main British port for Shetland, and it is just as far from Lerwick as is Bergen.

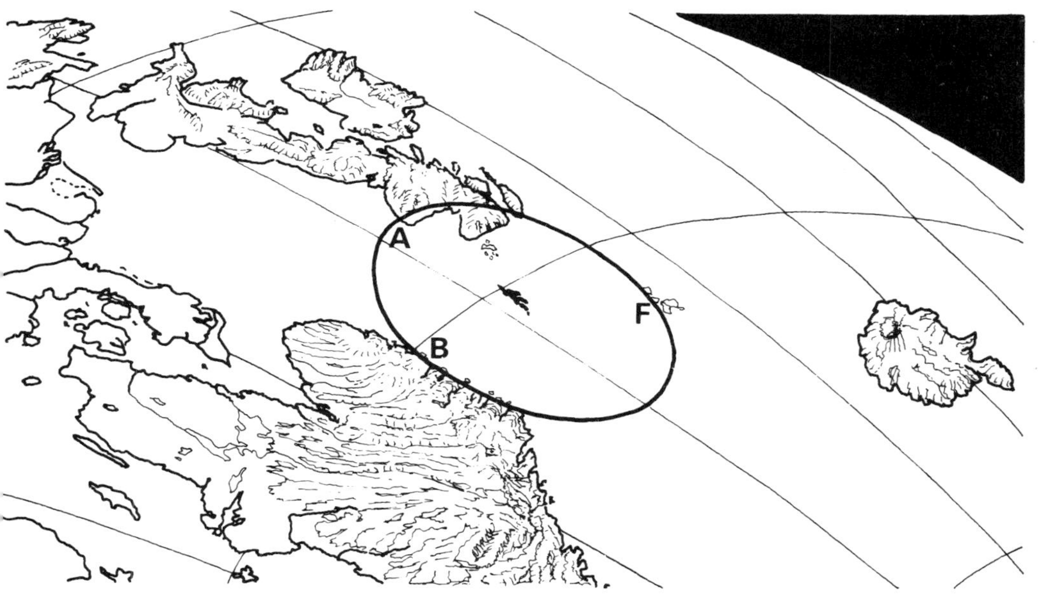

The radius of the circle centred on Shetland is 200 miles:
A: Aberdeen   B: Bergen   F: Faroes

The distance from the Lerwick harbour mouths to the sea end of the channel into Bergen through the Norwegian islands can be run in a day or a night in a modern vessel, while with favourable winds it need take no more than two days under sail. It is about two hundred miles. In practice in reasonable weather the distance out of sight of land is often little more than half this, between the time when the top of Ronas Hill (at almost 1500 feet the highest in Shetland) drops below the horizon, and the tops of the mountains of Norway appear. Long before the days of modern electronic direction finding, passage-makers had bad weather navigation methods that freed them from dependence on these landmarks. In the days of sail fishing boats, and one may suspect in the Viking period too, seamen cultivated the ability to read the wave pattern so that they could find their way by it when visibility was low. Men caught by fog or a gale when fishing off the coast of Norway faced the risk of missing the Shetlands altogether and being carried out into the Atlantic. However they often proved their ability to follow the "moder-dai", that is the underlying scend to the waves imparted by the coast and seabed topography within soundings. They could use this as a guide homewards even when it was disguised by interaction with wave components generated by the wind and the run of the tide.

It is not unknown for the crossing to Norway to be made even by Shetlanders with no pretensions as navigators, in very small boats, and sometimes quite unintentionally! For example, there is a story from Unst (the most northerly of the main Shetland islands) about two girls who set out in a little rowing boat to milk a cow that was being kept on a small island offshore. A squall blew up, and they were not seen again. Eventually, to the shame of the men of Unst, it transpired that they had been blown to Norway and had preferred to settle and marry there rather than return. That particular tale may be apocryphal, but other cases, like that of Betty Mouat, are well established. On 30th January, 1886, she left Grutness near the south tip of Shetland (see Chapter 7) on the sailing cutter *Columbine* to go up to Lerwick to sell socks she had knitted. The skipper was washed overboard, and the mate and the ship's boy went after him in the dinghy. They lost touch with the cutter, which by then had only Betty aboard. The sixty-year-old lady was trapped in the cabin, but four days later *Columbine* delivered her safely in Norway. Unlike the Unst lasses she returned, coming via Newcastle by steamer. It is said that there her basketful of fine Shetland socks fetched twice what she would have got for them in Lerwick . . .

But perhaps the best of these stories was one told to Ian Morrison over a dram by friends at Vidlin, in the north-east of Shetland. It concerns one Sandy Sutherland, of a generation long since departed. At the time of the story he was a young man, and but newly married.

He was out fishing one day in a very small 'eela' boat, with his lines down "out by east", between Vidlin and the Out Skerries. Fog closed down. He had no compass, but was not unduly worried. He had taken note of the wind direction, and by it he shaped course for home. Unbeknownst to him, when the fog had closed in the wind went right round so that instead of heading the short distance west to Vidlin Voe, he ran eastwards, out past the Skerries, without sighting them in the haar. Eventually, despite the tiny size of his craft, he contrived to land safely on the coast of Norway. There he was befriended by a "Norrawa Finn Wyfe".

So far, the story had been prosaic enough, but now it took on a new dimension, as the glint in the eye of the lady telling it and in the eyes of her assembled kinsfolk warned even a Sooth-Moother. In Shetland lore, the Finn-folk are not mundane inhabitants of the immaculate glass-and-concrete world of Helsinki, but denizens of a more shadowy troll-ridden land who have special powers over wind and sea.

Sandy was not keen to attempt the return crossing in his little cockle-shell of a boat. But he was very worried about what would happen to his new bride, if he was given up for lost at sea. The sea witch offered to fly over to Shetland in a night to see how the girl was faring. When she arrived, she changed herself into a dog, the better to observe. What she saw confirmed Sandy's fears. The girl's in-laws had no desire to be saddled with a young widow, and she was back living with her old mother, in great poverty. Despite this, being a kindly lass she gave a piece of her scant stock of meat to the hungry looking dog that had suddenly appeared at her door. The dog quietly made off with her knife from the table, and next day, once more in Norway and in the guise of a Finn-wyfe, gave this to Sandy as a token of the accuracy of her report. He recognised his wife's knife, and decided that he could wait for a ship no longer, but must try to sail home even though his own tiny craft was all that was available to him. Seeing and approving his determination, the Finn took his red sailor's kerchief, and showed him how to knot the four corners to control the sea and winds. He followed her instructions implicitly: he loosed the first corner as he left the Norrawa strand; the second as he dropped the mountains of Norway below the horizon; the next as he raised Ronas Hill over the western horizon; and the last as he reached Vidlin. Soon he had set all to rights, and he and his wife lived out their days in happiness.

This story was introduced partly on the principle that the judicious reader is never averse to a good yarn, but also because it illustrates the common ground in the cultural heritage of the Shetland and Scandinavian worlds. Finns with magic knots, trolls and trowies, sealmen and sealwomen, fire rituals at mid-winter, with pagan-Viking allusions; there are many cases. Some further samples of this will be illustrated shortly along with other examples from what seems an extraordinary variety of parallels, ranging (as noted in Chapter 1) from place-names to fiddle tunes.

It appears less extraordinary when one realises that it is not merely a matter of geographical proximity, but that historically Shetland remained a political part of the Scandinavian world not just until the end of the Viking period, but until the end of the Middle Ages. The islands were thus in Scandinavian hands for rather longer than the length of the period that they have been considered a part of Scotland. By the time the islands came to the Scottish crown in 1469, the type of world that one associates with the Vikings was thus long past. People alive then had seen or were to live to see not Viking raids on Iona or Jarrow but the taking of Constantinople by the Turks, or the Christian reconquest of Spain and the expulsion of the Moors. The Hundred Year's War had just come to an end, and although the English were in the midst of the Wars of the Roses, and Scotland was no less turbulent, this was also the period of Michelangelo's work for Lorenzo de Medici in Florence, and of the development of books printed with movable type. When King Christian I of Denmark and Norway wrote to his subjects in Shetland on 28th May, 1469, and told them to do homage to the Scottish King James III and pay their taxes to him, almost half a millennium had elapsed since Bjarni Herjolfsson sighted the unknown lands southwest of Greenland that Leif the Lucky named Vinland. In contrast, less than a quarter of a century remained before Columbus was to sail.

Even in 1469, it was not clear that the transfer was a permanent one. Shetland, like the neighbouring Orkney islands the previous year, had merely been pledged against the dowry due to the Scottish crown for the marriage of Margaret, Christian's daughter, to James. Some ramifications of this have reached towards the present day. Thus, even in recent years there have been test cases in Scottish courts regarding the Norse legacy of Udal law in Shetland. This ancient system has been largely abolished in Norway now, but neither Scottish nor British parliaments have ever got around to doing this formally for Shetland. Historians have argued over whether the relinquishment of the islands was a matter of premeditated policy for Christian, or merely one of expediency and shortage of ready cash. Be that as it may, the mortgage omits to set a time limit for the redemption of the islands, a fact of which some Shetlanders take joy in reminding Whitehall.

For example, recently when something as mundane as the creation of a new Water Board based on the northerly counties of the Scottish mainland but including the northern isles went before Parliament, "Back to Norway" slogans appeared in Shetland. This was undeniably tongue-in-cheek, but equally certainly there is local awareness that Norway despite her limited resources seems to have handled the problems of remote areas more successfully than successive British governments. Shetlanders have good practical grounds for suspecting the viability of plans such as that proposed in the Wheatley report. This suggested that for local government purposes the islands should be grouped with an enormous and essentially westerly region of the Scottish Highlands. For most practical purposes, Shetland communicates with mainland Britain through Aberdeen and the east not west coast, and anyway as the islanders were quick to point out the southerly limit of the proposed region was as near to south-east England as it was to them. More recently, the validity of special all-purpose authorities for Shetland and Orkney has been recognised in a government white paper of 1971.

In the eyes of some Shetlanders, this still does not go far enough. They note that the Faroe Islands, considerably further out into the North Atlantic than they are, have more than doubled their population while that of Shetland has halved. The Faroes have autonomy under the Danish crown, and some Shetlanders around the time of the five hundredth anniversary of the transfer in 1969, made the gesture of petitioning Queen Elizabeth to honour alleged undertakings of James III to preserve a separate administration in the islands. They felt it typical that the discovery, during the preparation of the petition, of a little known text of the Shetland contract of 1469 was headlined by Norwegian newspapers to a notably greater extent than by southern British ones.

It is of course very easy to indulge in historical romanticism, and read more into all this than any Shetlander would. They are not Scandinavian now. It is merely that they are cheerfully aware that they are neither Highland Scots nor Lowland Scots, let alone Englishmen!

Language is often taken as one of the key diagnostics of nationality, and in the case of Shetland it certainly provides hints about the pattern underlying the islanders' perception of their regional identity. Thus, although there may be a greater demand for detective stories in Norwegian than in most county libraries in Britain, the basic language of Shetland has not been a Scandinavian one for a very long time now. It seems that within about a century of the political union with Scotland many Shetlanders were bilingual, speaking their old Norn language amongst themselves but understanding the official Scots of the courts and implanted church. Business documents in the old Viking-derived tongue fade out by about the time that Shakespeare was writing his last plays six hundred miles to the southward. On the other hand, although Lowland Scots and then English have been coming in for more than four hundred years, the process has been one of assimilation rather than decisive extirpation of the Norse language. Within the childhood of people still alive today, Dr. Jakob Jakobsen noted ten thousand Scandinavian words still in use in Shetland. Many of these were falling out of use then, and more have since. However, as the members of the Expedition found, the everyday speech of schoolchildren as well as grandmothers still maintains the tradition in a lively and pleasantly "non-antiquarian" way in the nineteen-seventies.

It is hardly surprising that the Shetlanders have managed to evolve their own regional culture, assimilating influences from the south rather than being swamped by them. Their proximity to south Norway has already been noted: there are further aspects of this. The most densely populated and influential parts of Scandinavia both at present and in the past have been the southern parts. Broadly speaking, the same is true of the British Isles. The difference lies in the relative position of these southerly zones relative to Shetland: the islands are juxtaposed to the more populous end of Scandinavia, but lie off the least populous part of Great Britain. Those of the Expedition who flew north from Edinburgh over the Scottish Highlands were impressed by the scale of the bleak wastelands crossed on the way to Shetland. Two of the Americans said that they had had no idea that so big "empty areas" existed in the United Kingdom.

Shetland is 300 miles from Edinburgh and 600 miles from London. Within two lifetimes of the transfer of Shetland to the Scottish crown, James VI of Scotland also became James I of England, and took his court south from Edinburgh to the English capital. In little more than a century, the union of the Parliaments followed, and government was centralised even more firmly in London, a city that is as near to Milan, Marseilles, Berlin or Bilbao as

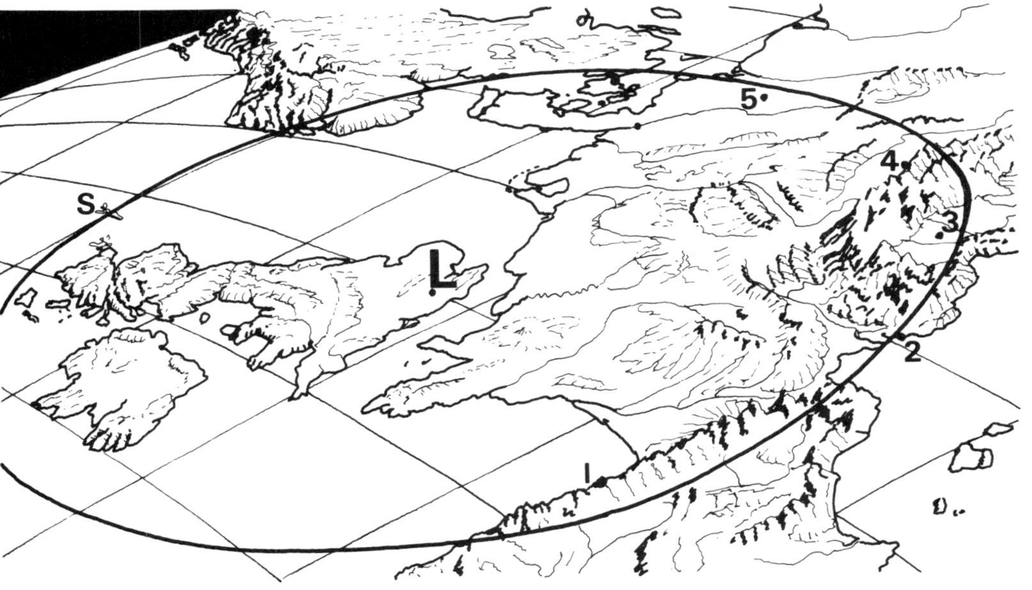

L: London S: Shetland
1: Bilbao 2: Marseilles 3: Milan 4: Munich 5: Berlin

it is to Lerwick. Sometimes, to Shetland eyes this shows, even today. Remembered past deficiencies of central government, and old history about incoming landlords and churchmen and their exactions, perhaps have had a role in fostering the climate of independent enterprise that impressed the Expedition members. There is a Shetland saying that in the past nothing but dear oatmeal and greedy ministers ever came from the south. Certainly the virtue of making one's own opportunities has been emphasised for the Shetlanders in recent years by the way that they have contrived to prosper by expanding their fishing, agriculture and knitwear industries, even during the recession of the early nineteen seventies when many other areas of the United Kingdom suffered heavy unemployment. The Highlands and Islands Development Board has played a significant part by providing capital backing in recognition of the local initiative.

In the last twenty years, the Shetlands have changed from rundown islands to a prospering community that can literally afford to weigh the loss of amenity that involvement with the North Sea oil industry would entail against the economic advantages that it might bring. The decline in population evident over the last century has been reversed. In this economic revitalisation, the extent to which Scandinavian rather than southern British approaches have been considered is an indication of the extent to which the Shetlanders still consider themselves a part of a world centred in northern seas. Their reasons are practical and economic, rather than merely sentimental or antiquarian. Working parties have been sent to Faroe and to Norway to study their economic and social techniques for combating depopulation. These have influenced the Shetland policy of concentrating resources and amenities to develop selected major villages as well equipped holding points and ultimately regional growth points for population. At an early stage in the planning, when the desirability of a rise in population was recognised and the encouragement of immigration was considered, a serious suggestion was made that the incomers should come from Scandinavia. The urban-minded Scots of the south seemed less likely to succeed with the practical problems of sea and land in Shetland.

There is thus as much geography as history in Shetland's Scandinavian links and parallels. There are Scandinavian place-names in plenty in the English Midlands in the areas of the old Danelaw, but travelling there today it takes a substantial effort of imagination to conceive any connection with Norse landscapes and seascapes. In Shetland on the other hand, one can not but be conscious of being in a high-latitude archipelago, girt by northerly seas. Those of the Expedition who had been in Iceland sometimes had a strange feeling of *déja vue*. The road, winding through a moor bleak with peat hags and blowing bog cotton, would suddenly breast a rise, disclosing a tall flat-topped headland with skerries offshore, and long low croft houses sheltering amid narrow fields in a hollow above the storm beach.

The Norse aspect of the Shetland landscape goes deeper than the imprint of man upon it. Even the rocks making up the islands are very much like those of much of Norway. They are as ancient, and have been wracked by the same history of mountain building and erosion. Indeed, because of basic geological differences between Denmark and Norway, it is much easier to find parallels between Shetland and Norwegian scenery than between that of Denmark and Norway. In Shetland as in Norway, the differences in hardness and the fault lines in the old rocks have been picked out by the glaciations of the last few million years. There are indeed indications that Norwegian ice itself reached Shetland. A large erratic boulder deposited in south Shetland has been identified as coming from an outcrop near Oslo.

It is not only the traces of glaciation that remind the visitor to the islands of their northerly position. The advance party of the Expedition arrived a few days after mid-summer's day, and found that they were in a land virtually without night. Although not quite far enough north to qualify for the Midnight Sun, Shetland's summer regime is far from what the inhabitants of London or New York, respectively some 10° and 20° further south, consider normal. Instead of any real darkness, there was only "da simmer dim", a period of bright twilight in which one had no trouble in reading small print out of doors at midnight. Even as the two months of the Expedition drew on and night came back, the northern latitude meant that the darkness was often enlivened by displays of the aurora borealis. On one particularly memorable occasion, divers on a night operation came up through water glowing with phosphorescence to find the whole sky draped with shifting sheets of aurora borealis. The coin falls on its other side in the winter however, with the days getting shorter and shorter until on mid-winter's day itself the sun is below the horizon for more than eighteen of the twenty-four hours, and in Lerwick many of the benighted inhabitants press through the streets waving flaming brands and Viking axes . . . but more of this shortly.

The latitude that brings about this seasonal contrast is indeed a high one. New York lies around 41°N, London about 51°N, while Shetland is mostly between 60 and 61°N. The Arctic Circle at 66½°N is as near to Shetland as Shetland is to Newcastle or Belfast. The islands thus lie north of Stockholm, let alone Malmo, Copenhagen or Riga. Moscow is far to the south. Indeed they are well north of such snow-bound places as Churchill on Hudson's Bay, Juneau in Alaska, the Aleutians and most of the Bering Sea. They share the same latitude with not only Bergen and Oslo, but Helsinki, Leningrad, much of Siberia and even Cape Farewell at the tip of Greenland.

This perhaps explains a clause that some Expedition members noticed in the small print of their diving insurance policies, some time after arriving in Shetland. The policies covered all manner of risks, particularly for British waters, but excluded anything that might happen beyond 60°N or S. Clearly they had in mind divers being crushed by pack ice or gnawed by polar bears. Nothing quite so dramatic seemed likely to happen to the team, but it seemed advisable to check whether the 60° exclusion applied within Britain too. Phone calls to offices far to the south were greeted with blank disbelief that any part of Britain could lie so far north. Eventually it

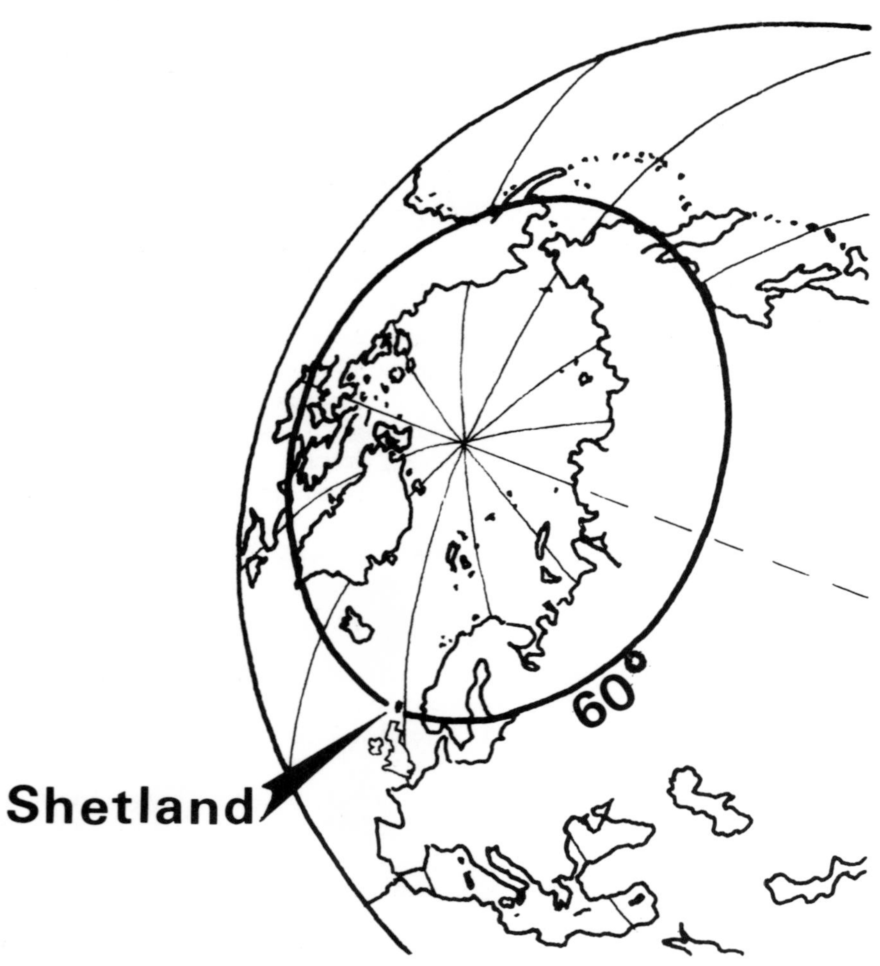

Shetland and 60° Latitude line

seemed simplest to accept that any carcasses should be allowed to drift ashore only at Sumburgh Head, where the southernmost tip of Shetland crossed the magic line and reached towards 59° 50′N. Happily, all survived and no claims had to be made.

What the insurance company's 60° ruling failed to allow for was the fact that climatic zones are not simply latitudinal. The effects of continental masses and ocean circulation have to be taken into account. Most of the other northerly places quoted in the latitude comparison are subject either to continental effects or cold ocean

Above: *Auskerry*

Right: *Kaeb and humlabund*

Ness Yole

currents, and have severe winters. Shetland on the other hand is in the track of moderating westerly winds coming in across the ocean, which is here warmed by the North Atlantic Drift. This is the northward continuation of the Gulf Steam. The result is an equable climate, with winter temperatures almost the same as those of Edinburgh or indeed London. In fact the winters are altogether less severe than in Chicago, or New York State where some of the team lived. Although so far to the southward, these can be subject to harsh continental effects. The moderating influence of the ocean sadly also keeps the summer temperatures fairly low in Shetland (in July at 12°C, about 3°C cooler than Edinburgh, or 6°C cooler than London). During the Expedition however the weather was generally rather better than average. Cloud cover when present was usually thin and several members of the Expedition developed rashes that the doctor ascribed to excessive exposure to ultraviolet radiation during the long days.

The Expedition took place during the calmest part of the year, and to those whose previous work in Shetland waters had been around the Equinoxes, the contrast was startling. There were days on end with the sea like a millpond, and underwater visibility could be superb. The water cleared until sometimes the divers felt like birds flying in bright blue air. Those who had worked on the wreck of *Liefde* off the Out Skerries in the autumn were more used to a Shetland where one did one's diving between gales, and often felt wave motion plucking gently but insistently ten fathoms down.

The islands are wide open to gales. The wind can blow unimpeded all the way across the Atlantic from Labrador, or right down out of the Arctic. For eight months in the year, the *average* wind speed does not drop below 15 m.p.h., and through December, January and February it stays over 20 m.p.h. There are between two hundred and two hundred and fifty hours of full gales per year, and some of the highest windspeeds known in Britain have been recorded in Shetland. A gust registered at 177 knots at RAF Saxa Vord, Unst, but it took the head of the anemometer off downwind with it, so no one is quite sure what speed it really reached! During the gales, salt spray is whipped into the air. It can give astonishing winter sunsets, but as much as the winds themselves, the salt may contribute to the difficulty of growing trees on Shetland. At present there are only a few small plantations, well inland. The Shetlanders take "microclimatic countermeasures" by building plantie krubs, little stone walled enclosures to shelter their cabbage seedlings. Out of cabbage season, these serve other purposes. During gales in the Out

Skerries, the *Liefde* divers sometimes saw one covered with a cargo net, well weighted down with boulders. Inside were rammed the crofter's chickens, murning and clucking. On days like that, when men had difficulty in keeping their feet in the gusts and the thoughts of divers turned to lead boots for use on land, this seemed the only way to prevent the chooks from ending up salt-pickled in Bergen.

Although the islands are by no means as arctic as their latitude might lead one to expect, the Shetlands are thus certainly rugged, and lie in northern seas that can on occasion provide severe tests for seamanship. They were attractive to Scandinavians during the Viking era partly as a stepping stone to points west or south, and partly we may suspect because they offered a place to settle where the habitat and resources were similar to much of Norway, and the problems, too, of land and sea were ones with which they could deal familiarly. We will shortly take a closer look at some of the aspects of Shetland life that reflect the Scandinavian links of Viking and later times, but a caveat is necessary before embarking on this.

The danger here, of course, is that by stressing archaic elements surviving in the present "Shetland way-of-life" and the folk culture of the recent past, one may give the impression that these are museum islands, peopled by quaint folksy folk. Nothing could be further from the truth. A taste for wind-dried fish may be rooted far back in the islanders' past, but at Sumburgh one is likely to see fish drying in the airy shelter of so modern a structure as an aircraft hangar. The men who caught them are certainly neither "ignorant peasants" nor "antiquarian gastronomes". They spend their spare evenings fishing in the Voe in yoles with beautiful Viking shapes but by day they look after helicopters. These are of the type used for recovering astronauts on splash-down, here used for swapping crews on the offshore oil-rigs. The airport men wind-dry the fish because they *like* them that way; and the boat-type is one that has been developed to be just as effectively adapted to its function as is the helicopter to its role.

The Viking elements in present day Shetland boats will be discussed further in a later chapter; the point here is that where the legacy of the past has survived, there has generally been a good reason for this: functional, economic or in terms of established taste. In many ways, the functional and economic constraints have changed more in the last fifty or hundred years than they had up to then since Viking times, and for that reason much of what follows refers to things familiar to Shetlanders but relating to their parents or grandparents day. In other cases, traditional skills have flowered and developed in this century because new economic outlets have arisen, or been created. Sealskin or sheepskin working are superficially "ethnic" industries of this kind but the production of Shetland knitwear is the example par excellence. It may be still to a large extent a cottage industry, but outside the cottages stand the shiny new cars of the knitters . . Furthermore, these same cars are likely to be seen parked among the peat banks, being loaded with polythene sacks of fuel that have been cut with a *tuskar.* The name, like the

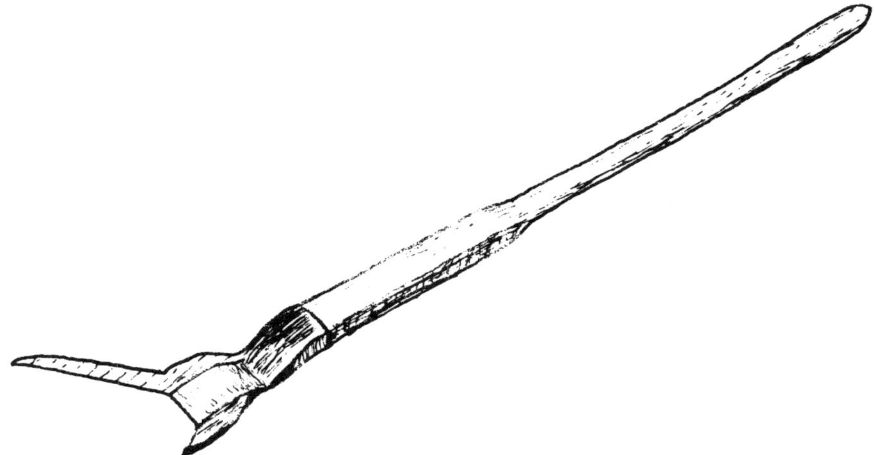

Tuskar

very practical implement itself, is a survival of the Old Norse torfskeri or peat spade, but it is a measure of the Shetlands in the seventies that Expedition members were actually startled to see peats being fetched home by pony on the island of Yell, so used had they become to seeing well polished Rovers or Volvos bearing loads in for Lerwick families. Clearly, from the cars they were running, for many of the Shetlanders the freight rates for alternative fuels are secondary to the pleasant flame and scent of a peat fire.

Tastes for wind-dried fish or peat fires are not a mark of the islanders' insularity, favoured because they know nothing else. There is a story about a Sooth-Moother tourist who told an aged man in Shetland about the delights of Aberdeen, in some detail. The old lad listened courteously, but there was a glint in his eye as he replied, "Mebbe so, but it's no a patch on Rio, or Macao come to that. . ." Lerwick itself often has a distinctly cosmopolitan air, for Norwegians, Danes and Faroese are by no means the only fishermen to call in. Most European nations have some vessels passing through. Supply tankers come to get water for the Russian fleet, and English and Scots mingle with fishermen of Germany East and West, Poland, France, the Low Countries and even Israel. The coming of the oil rig tenders, some even with the traditional Texans among their international crews, has merely augmented the flow. It has certainly not started anything new. Lubeckers and merchants from Hamburg competed with Bergen traders and Hollanders in Shetland from the days of the Hanseatic League onwards. A sixteenth century tombstone in Unst tells in German how one Segebad Detken, burger of Bremen, had carried on his business in Shetland for no less than 52 years. Half a century later, Sandwick Bay was being referred to as "Hamborgh Haven" and the Pool of Virkie (see Chapter 8) as the Dutch Pool, while even in living memory the island of Whalsay had its Bremen Strasse.

It is not only that foreigners have come to fish or trade in Shetland. The traffic seems always to have been two-way. Even in the thirteenth century, place names like "Hialtbyr" (from the Old Norse "Hjaltland" for Shetland) tell of settlements of Shetlanders across in Bohuslan at the junction of Skagerrak and Kattegat, and later Shetland settlers were common particularly in the fishing districts of the Norwegian coast. There were certainly Shetlanders living as 'borgers' of Bergen in the 16th and 17th centuries.

Even home-based Shetlanders tend to have seen more of the world than most Britishers. The tradition of seamanship in the islands, rooted in the Viking age but kept active by the everyday exigencies of living in the archipelago and fishing the waters around it, has led a high proportion of Shetland men into the Royal or Merchant Navies at some time in their careers. One measure of the level of this involvement, though a sad one, is the fact that the county lost by death in the two World Wars the highest percentage of males of any British county. In war as in peace, Shetland men have served on most of the world's oceans.

Again, the pattern is an old one. The prime seamen of Shetland were in high demand for the Navy during the Napoleonic Wars and earlier and the islands often suffered from the excesses of the Press Gangs. Throughout the 18th and 19th centuries the Arctic whalers from Hull, Whitby, Dundee, Aberdeen or Peterhead put into Lerwick on their way north, relying on Shetlanders to make up their crews. Besides being unequalled boat-handlers, they were reckoned to be steadier and less given to drunkenness than many of the Scots and English seamen. Be that as it may, Lerwick when the Greenland

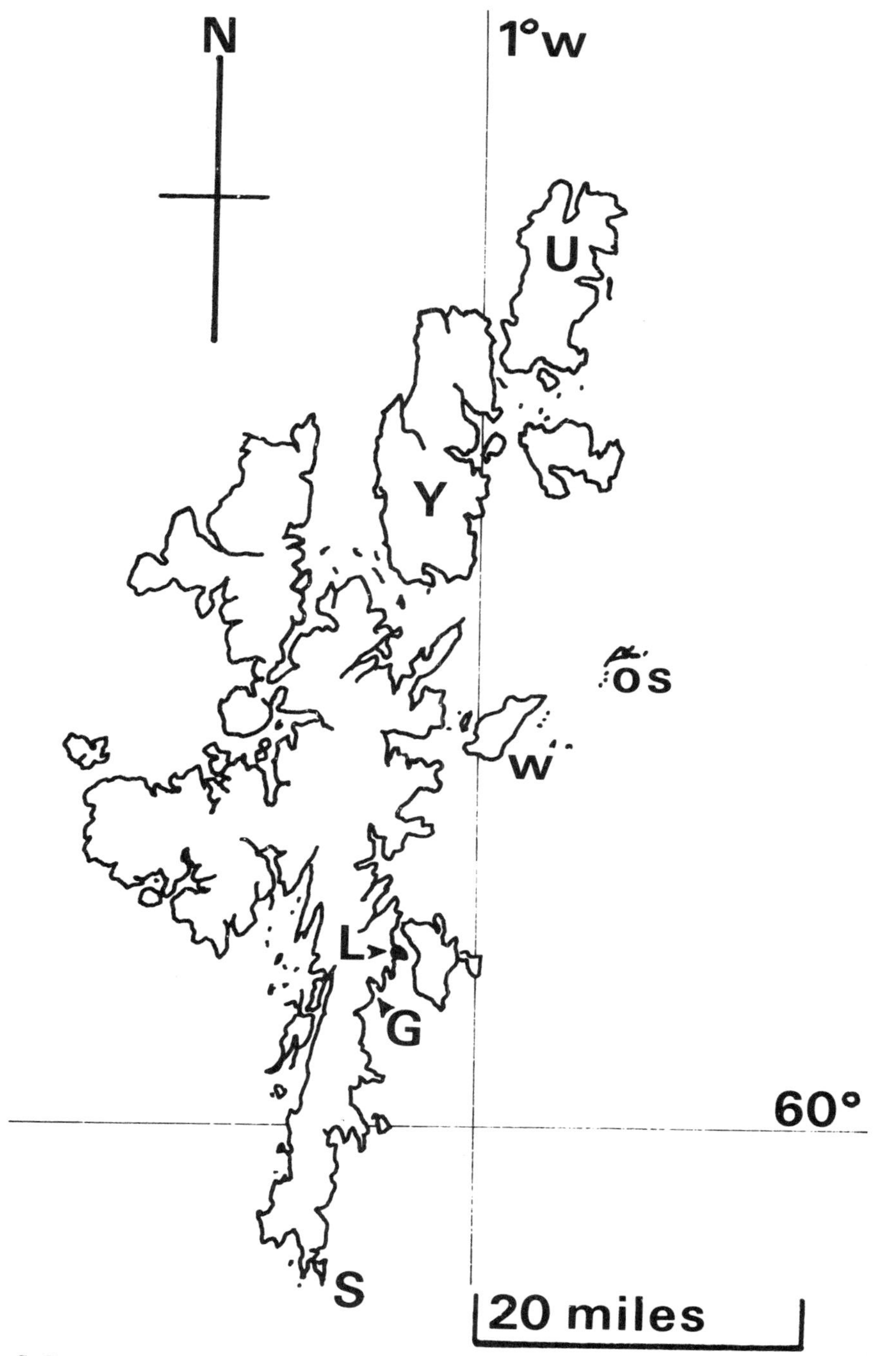

S. Sumburgh G. Gulberwick L. Lerwick W. Whalsay OS. Out Skerries Y. Yell U. Unst.

A reconstruction of 18th century Lerwick

whalers passed through was known for the hell-raising in its grog shops, and even in the late days as many as fifty special constables might be enrolled to contain them. When Sir Walter Scott visited the town in 1814, he came forth with the following slightly prim lines:

Here's to the Greenland tar, a fiercer guest
Claims a brief hour of riot, not of rest;
Proves each wild frolic that in wine has birth,
And wakes the land with brawls and boisterous mirth.

When the whaling shifted to Antarctic waters in the present century, to the very last the crews of the British-owned vessels were dominated by Shetlanders and Norwegians. Indeed, the capacity of the Shetland seamen to cope with the tougher jobs afloat, combined with the shortage until quite recently of alternative work within the islands, led to their becoming so ubiquitous throughout the merchant seaways of the world that in the days of the British Empire they were sometimes referred to as "North Sea Chinamen" – though probably not to their faces! The tourist's old seaman, with his memories of Rio and Macao was thus anything but exceptional, and often Shetlanders proved rather better travelled and more cosmopolitan than many a Londoner or New Yorker.

The sea has thus remained as it was in Viking times, as much a highway as a moat for the islanders. Against this background let us now look more closely at some of the aspects of the Scandinavian legacy to the islands that the Expedition members found particularly intriguing.

Perhaps chief among these was the Shetland dialect. It will be recalled that we were ourselves a broad-spoken crew, with the Lowland Scots tongue mingling with Bronx and Bradford; prime Geordie with the sharpness of Chicago and the scrumpie-mellowed cadences of the West Country. Only the Londoners held that they spoke a "non-regional" English, and the rest of us took leave to doubt that. But all were agreed that the Shetland tongue was something special.

Those who had been in the Scandinavian countries sometimes got a strange feeling that they were back there. Shetlanders talking among themselves, if half-heard so that only the speech rhythms register, can sound distinctly Scandinavian in their pronunciation and accentuation. Dr. Jakob Jakobsen of Copenhagen noticed this too when he came over to study the Shetland dialect eighty years ago, and presumably it was even more marked then than it is now, after the standardising influence of radio and television.

In some parts of Britain, the regional speech is coming so close to a "lowest common denominator Standard English" that all awareness of its separate character has been lost. In Shetland however not only is the dialect maintained as a natural and lively medium for poets and prose writers, young as well as old, but awareness of its different rhythms and vocabulary is apparent in everyday transactions. Thus Expedition foragers, shopping in Lerwick or buying loaves for fifty at country bakeries, never ceased to be amazed at the adroit linguistic gear-changing that went on on the other side of the counter. Seeing strangers, the shopkeepers often addressed them in an English that was nearer to B.B.C. standards than many an Expeditionary could manage in return. They meantime kept up a cheery flow of asides to fellow Shetlanders, with an entirely different vocabulary and intonation . . .

Sometimes there was a bit of leg-pulling at our ignorance of the tongue. Coming up off the sands out of breath after some pulley-hauley beaching the diving boats, one was not sure just how complimentary the watching housewife was being when she commented that you were "blaain laek a neesik" – but if she added "Bide dee fir I spaek wi dese bairns – dere skreehin laek peerie swaabies", there was a fair chance that if you waited as instructed while she had a word with her children (sounding "like wee seagulls" in the background), then an invitation would follow for "a scar o' tae an twartree bannocks", to Sooth-Moothers, "a cuppa and two or three oatmeal cakes".

Sometimes no amount of guesswork would help if one did not know the dialect – or Old Norse. Consider the strange case of the njuggle-trouble at the County Museum. There is a working model there of the kind of Norse watermill that was widely used until the present century in the Northern Isles. Quite unlike the usual kind of watermill, it uses a turbine-like horizontal wheel, set on a vertical spindle. Something had gone wrong with the Museum one. It refused to turn when the button was pressed. The pump that recycled the water was checked, and found to be fully serviceable, indeed all visible working parts seemed to be in good order, but the mill remained recalcitrant. It was suggested, none too seriously, that since no other cause was apparent, this was evidently the work of "de njuggle". A Sooth-Moother might guess that this was some obscure mill-wright's term. He would be wrong. The word comes from Old Norse, and is used for the Shetland breed of what Scots call a Kelpie. That is a wraith in the form of a horse that lives in lochs and specialises in those branches of wickedness to do with water . . . and hence watermills. The Museum folk laughed, and got on with stripping the model right down. What they found was that its bearings were jammed . . . by a small horse. A peerie plastic horse. We can only hope that he was booty from some cornflake packet, insinuated into the mechanism by a crafty child well versed in folklore. The alternative is that the njuggles of the seventies have transformed themselves for the plastic age.

We shall return to Shetland's unnatural fauna shortly. Among the more natural kind, names derived from Norse sources are in very common use too, and many of the bird names in particular took the fancy of the amateur ornithologists in the Expedition team. A few of those that follow show Lowland Scots influence, some are direct onomatopoeia, and some are purely Shetland inventions, but the great majority are rooted in the old tongues of Scandinavia. One name refers to a bird no longer found in Shetland (Kliksi-Erne, the Whitetailed Eagle) and another form (Lingi Fugl) is an old one replaced now by the less euphonious "Lingi-bird". Otherwise the names are all known to Shetlanders at the present day, and many are very common usage indeed. But let them speak for themselves; try reading this out loud:–

Tanyick, Teetick, **Tirrick Tirrick**, Taang-Whaap;
Lingi-fugl, Mallimot, **Baagi Baagi**, Bonxie,
Tammi-Norie, Baaki-Craw, **Tystie Tystie**, Witchuk!
Dunter, Airlie, Lorin, Smirl –
Shalder, Solan, Scarf;
Longvie, Rindill, Kliksi-Erne –
Aalin, Maalie, Maa;
Pikkamaa, Pikkatari, **Plooti Plooti**, Alipooti,
Horra-Gös, Horni-Carp; **Kroga Kroga**, Catyogle;
Peerie-Swaabie, Ho-baagi, **Scorie Scorie**, Snippack!
Imber Snippack, Ebb-Snippet, Witchuk Witchuk, CRAA . . .

The English names that correspond respectively are:
Common Gull, Meadow Pipit, Tern, Whimbrel, Manx Shearwater, Fulmar, Great Blacked Gull, Great Skua, Puffin, Razor Bill, Black Guillemot, Sand Martin, Eider Duck, Bunting, Cormorant, Merlin, Oyster Catcher, Gannet, Shag or Cormorant, Guillemot, Wren, White-Tailed Eagle, Arctic Skua, Fulmar, Herring Gull, Kittiwake, Arctic Tern, Golden Plover, Stormy Petrel, Brent Goose, Puffin, Hooded Crow, Owl, Lesser Black Backed Gull (twice), Herring Gull, Snipe, Great Northern Diver, Dunlin and Hooded Crow.

Somehow in English they hardly seem to have as much character, and one can see why modern Shetland writers treasure the resources of the old tongue of the islands.

Here, as an example, is a fragment from a poem by Emily Milne about a cormorant. It addresses the bird with its dull grimy-looking coat, who still roots around the inlets in winter time when the others have left. He goes sneaking about amongst the seaweed along the tidelines "where many a butterfish, down thy throat, made his last earthly voyage". Accept the spelling as being phonetic, if no Shetlander is available.

Du Skarf, wi dull oonkirssen cott,
An ower-lang nebbit nose,
Du bedd aboot, i winter time,
Whin idders left da voes,
Smootin aboot, among da tang,
Closs ta da Shörmil edge,
Whaar mony a swaarfish, doon dy trot,
Made his last aertly vaige.

Cormorants

As it is with dialect words, so it is with place names. One can not but be aware that one is in a rather special part of Britain. For much of the time the Expedition base was in the Dunrossness Hall, near the southern end of Mainland Shetland. Motoring north from there each morning to the search areas in Gulberwick, the divers passed places with names such as Boddam, Troswick, da Ward o' Scousburgh, Cumlewick Ness, Longa Skerry, de Holm o' Helliness, Voxter, Fladdabister, or the East Voe of Quarff. They soon come to realise that wicks, voes, vaddles, houbs, and geos were all different categories of bays and inlets, named according to their breadth or the extent to which they dried out at low tide. In these as in the rest of the place names, the roots were almost invariably Old Norse. Thus the extraordinary sounding Fladdabister suddenly became comprehensible as "the steading on the flat ground", contrasting with Quarff, "a deep lying place, disappearing among the hills". Even Mavis Grind loses its overtones of Titus Groan, and becomes a precise description as "the gate of the narrow isthmus" in Norse. There are still tank traps there, to show that the notion of a gate at that slim pass, between St. Magnus Bay with the Atlantic to the west and Sullom Voe with the North Sea to the east, was as much in evidence in the wars of this century as in Viking times. Much of the diving took place below the farm of Setter in Gulberwick, and this had nothing to do with red dogs but came from the Old Norse for a dwelling in pastureland.

The Scandinavian links of the islands are not less marked if one turns from the names in the landscape in general to the names of things around an individual croft house. In recent decades the way of life that the traditional croft reflected has fast become obsolete in Shetland, as in Scandinavia. However, the parallels in the names for the most detailed parts of the buildings, and for the equipment for the activities that went on in and around them, reflect in a quite striking fashion the way in which much of the hardware of the crofters' world in both Shetland and Scandinavia at the start of the 20th century would have occasioned little surprise amongst their Viking forebears of the 10th century.

The survivals indicated by the names for house features have in fact been used by archaeologists to help in their reconstruction of Norse dwellings, such as the houses of the Jarlshof settlement described in Chapter 6. Details are given by J.R.C. Hamilton in the report on the excavations there. Not only the terms for major items like rafters, roof purlins, tie beams and thatch (langbands, ovi, vaggel and tekk) came from Old Norse. Even the names for very minor features, like the doorlatch and its attachment (de jok and wev), used by the grandparents of the present generation of Shetlanders, would have been more intelligible to Vikings than they are to Sooth-Moothers. The same is certainly true of the ringaloddi on the orn: the pot on the hearth.

Out of doors we have already seen that a peat spade is a tuskar, from the Old Norse torfskeri. In the same way, Norse roots account for okregord for an arable field and mildenstump for the tool for smoothing the ground after sowing, as well as explaining why grandfather tied his cow to a veggwol with a wolga. Des for stack, and gordsimmens for the ropes tying it down in the Shetland gales, have the same parentage. And so on.

It is not merely that the names have a Scandinavian ring. When an exhibition was held in 1969 at the time of the 500th anniversary of the transfer to Scotland, folk life material from the recent past of Shetland and Norway was placed side by side in the county museum. It proved essentially indistinguishable, so strong had been the common heritage and the continuity of later contacts reinforcing it.

Although many aspects of the crofting way of life have become obsolete or obsolescent, as indicated, this is far from true of the knitwear industry. This is on a thoroughly commercial basis, and though largely home-based and a part-time activity, has an annual

Shetlanders knitting and carrying peat

turnover ordinarily well over the million pound mark. The characteristic figure is no longer a lady hand-knitting with the needles stuck in the Shetland belt pad, as she walks home to the croft with a kishie of peats on her back, but a modern housewife with a big manually operated knitting machine. Beautiful hand-knitting is still done, but is certainly not as *commercially* viable as the machine work. The commercial realism is just as traditional as the patterns knitted, perhaps even more so. The islanders early found that the women folk could supplement the family income by selling knitwear off the island, and certainly by the 16th century considerable quantities were being sold through those German merchants mentioned earlier. The great Dutch fleets of herring busses brought customers in plenty in the 17th and 18th centuries, while in the Victorian era English interest grew. This century has seen important sales in America, while recently France has proved the largest customer outside Britain.

The characteristic "Shetland" or "Fair Isle" patterns have not remained static, but have been modified somewhat to match demand and fashion. There is a tale that crops up from time to time that elements in the patterns came to the islands via Spanish seamen from *El Gran Grifon*, a ship of the Spanish Armada wrecked on Fair Isle in 1588. *Grifon* certainly hit Fair Isle. Alan Bax worked with Colin Martin and divers of Naval Air Command SAC in surveying her remains. The link with the knitting patterns is however a very tenuous one, to say the least. The Spanish hypothesis is generally invoked to explain seemingly oriental motifs, but with Shetlanders sailing the seas of the world, it is surely at least as easy to envisage a local seaman bringing back a scarf, say, from the east as a present for his wife or mother, and the lady incorporating a motif borrowed from it in her knitting. Or perhaps the pattern may have travelled without need of a sample: during the Expedition, a large hairy diver from Tyneside who hardly seemed the type to spend his evenings knitting, was observed expertly transcribing Shetland patterns onto graph paper. It turned out that in his earlier days as a merchant seaman, he had collected patterns from all over the world and sent them home to keep the ladies of his family amused. Presumably this could have happened in Shetland too.

There is little doubt that like so much else in Shetland, the patterns are in fact basically Scandinavian in their affinities. And one does not have to cross the seas to make the comparison. The Shetlanders, besides exporting their own knitwear, import Norwegian and Faroese jerseys, and Norwegian snowflake patterns are often as common as native Shetland ones in the streets of Lerwick. For the very finest of knitwear however, one looks not to Scandinavia, but to such places as Unst where there is a tradition of knitting incredibly fine pure white lacy shawls and stoles. One of these, perhaps four square yards in extent, may only weigh a couple of ounces and it will flow easily through a wedding ring. They certainly cannot be machine made, and they are not casual purchases.

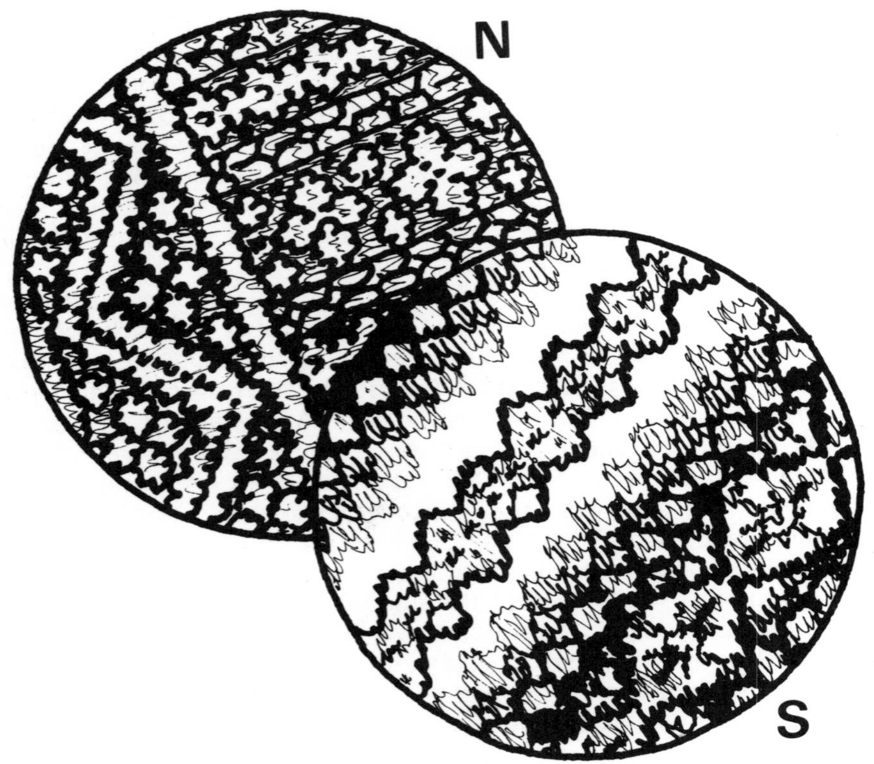

Patterns on jerseys bought in Lerwick
N: Norwegian S: Shetland

Another part of the traditional life of the isles that is happily thriving is music making, particularly fiddle playing. The Scottish fiddle tunes of Neil Gow or Scott Skinner are often heard in the islands, but the Shetland style of playing is in quite another idiom. It is one that is very much the islanders' own, and one which is still developing, with new tunes being added year by year. It is a measure of the liveliness of the Shetland culture that the businessman you meet in the bank, or the shopkeeper, shepherd or schoolmaster may turn out to be an active composer as well as player. There were few places indeed amongst all those in Britain and America from which the Expedition members came for which one could claim as much.

The Shetlanders themselves, if asked about the influences on their music, are apt to look the Sooth-Moother straight in the eye and tell him about the trowie tunes. That is, tunes learnt from "da peerie folk", the miniature trolls who live in the hollow hills. Fredaman Stickle, a German fiddler shipwrecked on Unst in the 18th century, is said to have got his tune *Da Trowie Burn* from them. With *Da Hens Mairch Ower de Midden*, *Craa dang Pussy*, or *Da Soo's Fareweel tae Tatties*, the fiddler is demonstrating his virtuosity while still keeping his tongue firmly in his cheek. But when he settles to playing some of the buoyant Shetland reels and wedding music, aspects of the style again place Shetland firmly at the Scandinavian end of the British spectrum. The closest parallel is perhaps with the Hardanger fiddle music of Norway, and one evening the comparison was made specific when off-duty divers found Mr. Tom Anderson of the Forty Fiddlers of Lerwick playing Norwegian tunes with his fiddle retuned Hardanger fashion: EAEA instead of EADG.

Most of the old dance steps with Norse rather than Scottish roots seem to have been lost, but there is a sword dance with pre-Reformation symbolism to a tune of notably Scandinavian character. This comes from Papa Stour, out in the Atlantic off the west coast of Shetland. Even in recent years, however, intriguing new musical material has come to light linking Shetland and Scandinavia. An Unst man, Mr. John Stickle, sang what he took to be a nonsense song for the collector Patrick Shuldham-Shaw. It ran:

> First you played the notes o' noy
> Scowan earl grey
> And then you played the notes o' joy
> For yetten kangra norla.

Mr. Shuldham-Shaw realised that he was hearing the lost tune belonging to words collected more than a hundred years ago on the same island, except that then the refrain had survived in a slightly less garbled form:

> Scowan orla grona
> Where gurtin grew for Norla

This was more easily identified with its Scandinavian original:

> Scoven aarlig grön
> Hvor hjorten han gaar aarlig

i.e.

> Yearly green is the wood
> Where the hart goes each year

The seeming nonsense was thus the last survival of a bi-lingual Shetland/Scandinavian ballad. Its verses tell how King Orfeo lost his Lady Isobel (or Lisa Bell) to the fairy folk, but won her back by charming them with his skill on the pipes. Its medieval pedigree is complicated, but ultimately it springs from the classical legends of Orpheus and Eurydice. So it seems that the tunnels where the trowies bide have far-reaching ramifications in the underworld . . .

From "earl grey" to "yearly green" is something of a riddle, and even today many Shetland riddles and proverbs have forms or wording that emphasise the Scandinavian connection. At the time of Jakob Jakobsen's visit at the end of last century, this was even more evident – what phenomenon, earthly or unearthly, is this?

Fira honga, fira gonga,
fira staad upo skø,
twa veestra vaig a bee,
and ane comes atta driljandi . . .

i.e., four hang, four go, four stand up towards the sky, two show the way to town, and one comes shaking behind. So the Shetland Norn runs, and the answer is nothing more outlandish than a milk cow (teats, legs, horns and ears, tail).

We have already encountered some of the less natural history of the islands, and in this as in much of their folklore the northern connections are again pervasive. The Shetland word selkie, for the seal, is another from Old Norse (sel-r) and the tales about seal men and seal women from Shetland illustrate the common heritage, for they form part of a pattern of stories that stretches from mainland Scandinavia through Faroe to Iceland. The stories are variations on the theme of seal people who come ashore in the guise of humans by taking off their pelts. Some lose the skin, and having had it returned to them by a mortal human, repay the favour at a later date, often by appearing as a seal in time to save the human from drowning. Others marry on land as humans, but despite attempts by the mortal spouse to keep the pelt hidden, eventually recover it and return to their own kind in the sea. Eric Linklater, the Orcadian author, has given a pleasant new twist to the tale of he who sings

"I am a man apo da Land
I am a Selkie in de sea"

by having a seal-man enrolled at Edinburgh University run off to sea

Gulberwick, looking south: with the headland of Setter Ness (where Fea Geo lies) on the left, and the bay head beach on the right.

Stava Geo, with the Hevdas fort on the headland, and the King's Knowe search area in the background

with one of the girl students.

This consciousness, and enjoyment, of the past in the present is one of the most striking things about the Northern Isles to the incomer. Yet, as has been emphasised, the islands house a shrewd and prospering modern community rather than a human museum. It is wholly consistent with the Shetland style that those most interested in the islands' past are often also those most involved in its present. This was certainly true of two of the Expedition's key contacts in Shetland, Captain William Inkster and Mr. Tom Henderson.

Captain Inkster is the harbourmaster at Lerwick, and something will already have been gathered of the range of international activity at that port. While the Expedition was in progress, we saw a vast oil rig enter Shetland waters at the end of a tow from the Gulf of Mexico. It was like encountering a peripatetic cathedral: it was difficult to grasp that a structure that size could be mobile, let alone manoeuverable, yet he "parked" it neatly in Bressay Sound as if this was the most routine piece of harbour business. Besides knowing his seamanship, however, he also knows his Sagas, and his views on points in them involving questions of seamanship, particularly in Shetland waters, are valued by scholars of more than one nation.

Tom Henderson is curator, and in many respects creator, of the lively County Museum in Lerwick. But although now professionally as well as by inclination involved with the conservation and exposition of Shetland's past, he can hardly be said to have retreated into it. On the contrary, he was County Convenor at the head of local government during the crucial period at the start of the nineteen-sixties when the economic revival of Shetland really got under way.

Consciousness of the rich Norse legacy in the islands is thus not incompatible with the businesslike outlook that the Expedition found typical among Shetlanders. The intensity of that consciousness, and the attitude to it, among Shetlanders of course varies. Home-made Country-and-Western music competes with Shetland reels; and while some delight in the Viking derivation of their Shetland-model racing craft, others are turning to class dinghies indistinguishable from those of the Solent.

The most overtly hindward-looking event of the Shetland year is Up Helly Aa, and this has illuminating aspects in more than one sense. On the evening of the last Tuesday in January, a thirty foot heraldic version of a Viking longship is dragged through the streets of Lerwick, escorted by a squad of Norse warriors brandishing swords and Viking axes. Sparks stream into the winter night from hundreds of tarry torches as the procession makes its way singing to open ground. There the Guizer Jarl leaves his steering oar, a trumpet sounds and the brands are heaved into the ship. As it burns, the crowd sing "The Norseman's Home". And that is just the start of the night.

The event embodies elements from Uphalliday, a pagan Norse Yule festival assimilated by the pre-Reformation church, and from fire rites with blazing tar rather similar to the "burning of the clavie" that still goes on on a dark mid-winter night at Burghead on the Moray Firth. The present form of Up Helly Aa, with the burning of the galley, emerged as recently as the last decade of the nineteenth century however. It is now firmly established as the chief spectacle of the island year.

In the present context, Up Helly Aa is interesting in two respects: its timing and its Viking emphasis. Although the date is a fairly arbitrary and recent selection from the range of the older festivals it reflects, it is significant that it has remained firmly out of the tourist season, though many summer visitors have wished that they could have seen it. Relatively recent though it may be, the festival can not be classed with the resuscitations of folk custom fostered elsewhere to boost revenue from tourism. There are never likely to be many holidaymakers around Lerwick in the last week of January. Up Helly Aa is essentially by Shetlanders, for Shetlanders. As the Provost of Lerwick put it to Her Majesty the Queen when she visited the islands on the quincentenary of their change of allegiance, "We rejoice in the sovereignty of Great Britain, but we cherish our earlier history".

This brings us to the final point necessary to this chapter. It is one illustrated by the specifically Viking emphasis of the festival. We have seen that contacts with Scandinavia have been continuous to the present day. They did not cease neatly in 1469, and certainly were not restricted merely to the Viking age. Yet it is the Viking phase that the Shetlanders celebrate. This chapter has made much of the Scandinavian legacy in the islands, and of the way that Shetlanders feel themselves to be distinct from other brands of British. Yet it would be wholly erroneous to conclude from this that they see themselves as second-string English-speaking outliers of present day Scandinavia.

One night on the Expedition when the grog was flowing between Shetlanders and Sooth-Moothers, this point was taken up. The Scots gave a toast, one with which they like to exasperate more numerous but lesser breeds, such as the English. It runs "Here's tae us – Wha's like us?" The Shetlanders there present went further, cheerfully declining to be associated even with Scots. They stressed the strength of their Viking strain. Reproached then with being reject Norwegians, tossed out of Scandinavia proper a thousand years before (the party by then was going well) they retaliated by explaining that the Norwegians left in Norway were no better than Scots or English: they were just the stay-at-homes left behind when the *real* Vikings sailed off in their longships to places like Shetland . . . Sentiments very like these have been heard to fall from the lips of Icelanders too, and one gathers that the Faroese have a similarly robust attitude to the Danes.

This independent viewpoint of the islanders is nothing new. It is evident in the Viking era itself. Even by the 11th and 12th centuries the islanders seem to have begun to regard themselves as something different from "Norwegians abroad". As F.T. Wainwright put it, they might look eastwards, "with affection perhaps, but not with the nostalgia of exiles". Scandinavian heritage and British sovereignty notwithstanding, in their own eyes the Shetlanders have thus been a distinct people since before the days of Earls Rognvald and Harald.

Let us now join the Earls in Bergen, and look at the immediate background of the events that led up to their shipwreck.

Chapter 3

The Earls Set Sail

The Expedition had its immediate roots in the meetings at Fort Bovisand, but in a very real sense it arose ultimately from discussions that took place eight and a quarter centuries earlier, in Bergen. In a way, those who brought it about were not Alan Bax, Jim Gill, Bob Farrell and Ian Morrison, but Ogmund and Erling, sons of a certain Wrinkly-Orm. It was they who set the events in train that brought about the wrecking of the Earls.

This was anything but their intention. They were powerful landed men, acting as counsellors to young King Ingi in Norway, and seeking to protect his interests and their own by fostering an alliance with Earl Rognvald. The precaution seemed very necessary. The situation in Norway was a potentially explosive one, for Ingi's father Harald Gilli had left more than one son, and Ingi though king was not the eldest. He had an older half-brother called Eystein, who was a bastard. For the moment, all was well, for most men with power found it convenient to defer to Ingi's legitimacy. The fact that he was still virtually a child and easily influenced no doubt contributed to this. Ogmund and Erling could see trouble ahead, with the possibility of rival factions adopting Eystein or perhaps Sigurd, a third and yet younger brother, as figurehead. *Orkneyinga Saga* tells us how they persuaded the young king to send an invitation to Rognvald to come and visit him in Bergen, and asked him to do his best to cultivate the Earl's friendship, so as to gain his backing if trouble developed between the brothers.

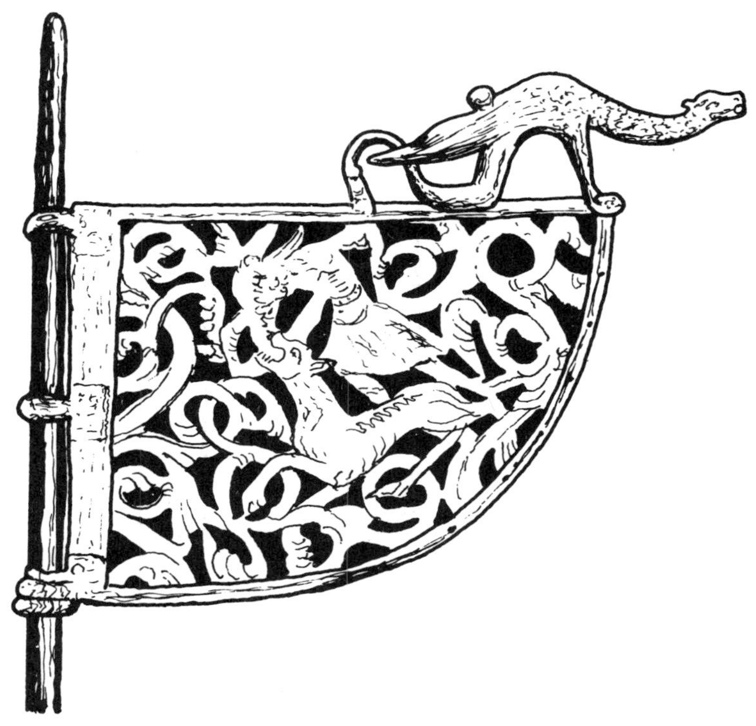

Viking ship's weather vane in gilt bronze; of the time of Hjolp *and* Fifa

It was well worth attempting, for Rognvald was no mere roving adventurer. He was a powerful magnate, with a large Norse realm in Orkney and Shetland. It must be remembered that this was late in the period we label "Viking" and there had been ample time for substantial Norse communities to develop there. It was over three and a half centuries since the westerly expansion of the Scandinavians really showed signs of getting under way. That is longer than the period between ourselves and the days of Charles the First.

Although the settlements in Orkney and Shetland were by then well established, this is not to say that life in them had become altogether peaceful. It was by no means devoid of the ruthlessness and off-hand violence that had been part of the earlier phases of the Viking expansion. *Orkneyinga Saga* gives a vivid picture of the complex jockeying for power in the islands. The axes are often out, warning beacons are sabotaged, and Rognvald only comes to the top after the elimination of his rival Earl Paul by Sweyn Asleif's son. Besides raiding on his own account as far afield as Wales, Sweyn aided Rognvald by kidnapping Paul and bearing him off to an obscure but apparently thoroughly grisly fate.

Rognvald's wary rival was by no means easy to ambush, and the ruse Sweyn used was as characteristic of the Viking style as any the Sagas tell of in earlier centuries. Earl Paul had gone out with a small retinue hunting sea otters for sport, at the foot of a headland in Orkney. Only a short excursion was in mind: the Saga tells us that

'cargo'

they meant to return home for their morning ale. They were never to drink it. Close inshore was what was apparently a merchant vessel, with only a small crew plying its sweeps. Its cargo of sacks was however Sweyn with his fighting men, lying hidden in their sleeping bags. Soon men and not otters were dying on the rocks, and the field was clear for Rognvald.

That happened in 1136, and by the time of King Ingi's invitation a dozen years later, Rognvald's faction had a secure grip on the islands and he was certainly worth seeking as an ally. He does not seem to have been displeased by the request to come to Bergen. He had apparently been a great friend of Ingi's father, and in any case according to the Saga he was eager to see kinsmen and friends in Norway. He quickly put preparations for the voyage in hand.

Earl Harald asked permission to accompany him. He was a lad of fourteen or fifteen then, and wanted to go along, as the Saga puts it, out of curiosity and for his own amusement. One version of the text describes him as "very stalwart" despite his youth. He was probably less than handsome, since by the time he was approaching twenty he was described as being an ugly man, though tall and strong. He was regarded as being no fool however, and even in his teens men thought him likely to emerge as a future leader.

The Saga tells us that Rognvald was a clean-limbed, well-made man of medium height, with light chestnut hair. It says that he was the most popular of fellows, and one of the most accomplished. We know however that the writer was biased in Rognvald's favour – as indeed was Rognvald himself! This is how the Earl described himself:

Master of draughts and nine kinds of sport;
Skilled at runes and at letters;
Skier, Archer, Oarsman,
I can play the harp,
Make verses, or fashion metalwork.

Be that as it may, they set sail in the early spring of 1148 with a fine retinue, and crossed to Bergen with a fleet of merchantmen. They got a warm welcome from King Ingi, and settled down to spend the summer visiting friends and kinsmen.

During this time, one Eindridi the Younger got back from Constantinople. The Saga says simply that he had been "in service" there for a long time, as though this was nothing unusual. Neither was it. Norsemen were by no means unknown around the Golden Horn and Bosphorus by then, and many served in the Varangian guard of the Byzantine emperors. Rognvald chatted frequently with him about what he had seen in his travels in the Levant, and Eindridi floated the idea of an expedition to the Holy Land to be led by the Earl.

The notion of a Viking Crusade may seem a contradiction in terms. Our image of the Norsemen still tends to be conditioned by the fulminations of monkish chroniclers and historians influenced by them. Even archaeological evidence tends to focus our attention on their pagan phase, for with the coming of Christianity burials become simple interments without the memorable grave goods of the era of Odin and Valhalla.

The pagan legacy was a rich one and lingered long, but already by the end of the tenth century King Olaf Tryggvason was ruthlessly opposing the old faith, and having pagans martyred in the name of Christianity. In the eleventh century the heathen religion faded fast before the organisation and strength of the Christians. In Scotland, it is difficult to find pagan graves in the Norse areas after the ninth century. The great Cathedral of St. Magnus at Kirkwall in Orkney was started soon after Earl Paul was supplanted, and it was Rognvald's father Kol who had most to do with financing and building it. It is thus less surprising than it perhaps seems at first sight that Rognvald listened to Eindridi's proposal with interest.

Erling, son of Wrinkly-Orm, seems to have seen the prospect of a joint expedition with Rognvald as an excellent way of cementing the alliance for which he had been angling. He spoke strongly in favour of the enterprise, and said he would join it if the Earl would agree to become leader. Rognvald was persuaded by this. Many other men of rank, seeing two such powerful figures coming together, decided to join with them.

To forestall divisive rivalry among the magnates taking part, it was agreed before preparations started that none of the ships involved, except the Earl's, should have more than thirty thwarts for rowers. His was also to be the only decorated ship. There was trouble over this later, when the expedition eventually left. Eindridi was to serve as guide, and though outranked by the others he seems to have been filled with his own importance as initiator of the expedition. First he delayed their departure, saying his vessel was not quite ready. Then when he finally appeared with it, it was a richly ornamented dragonship . . . and to compound his offence he proudly sailed past Rognvald's ship, when the rest of the fleet were courteously holding back in formation behind it. Pride comes before a fall however, and it is apparently with some glee that the Saga reports that while the rest came safe to Orkney, Eindridi's beautiful vessel hit Shetland and became a total wreck, and he had to send to Norway for a replacement. Sadly, no clue is given as to where divers might seek the dragon.

This is running ahead, however. After the arrangements of the expedition had been agreed in principle, preparations were put in hand. Rognvald commissioned John Limp-Leg to build a crusading ship for him in Norway, and charged him to take special pains over it. He certainly seems to have done that, for when it was finally delivered it was described in the Saga as a fine piece of workmanship, decorated all over with figurehead, stern and weather vanes inlaid with gold and the rest of the hull carved from stem to stern. It had thirty-five rowing benches.

Time clearly had to be allowed for preparations as lavish as this, and it was decided that the expedition should leave in 1150. Earl Rognvald therefore decided to sail home that autumn and spend the next two winters in his island realm.

It was at this point that King Ingi presented him with the ill-fated *Hjolp* and *Fifa* for his homeward voyage. Let us now try to picture what these vessels were like. In doing this, it will help to look not only at vessels of the Viking era itself, but at recent and present-day Shetland boats. These preserve aspects of the Viking style and construction method to a striking degree.

The description of the *Hjolp* and *Fifa* given in *Orkneyinga Saga* is tantalising in its brevity, but it is quite specific on several points. They were longships; rather small, very beautiful and especially made for rowing. It says that of all ships, they were the swiftest. This epithet need not be taken too literally (the Saga writer with similar grandiloquence describes the ship John Limp-Leg built for Rognvald as the most magnificent of *its* kind). Nevertheless, the general implication is clear. These are not burdensome ocean-going vessels of the hafskip or knarr type that were used for shifting cargoes out to Iceland. Those were stoutly built, high freeboard ships that seem to have operated essentially under sail. While sweeps were carried on them, and would often be used for manoeuvering in constricted waters, they were not basically rowing vessels. *Hjolp* and *Fifa,* on the other hand, we may safely envisage as long, low, slim and sweet-lined craft, constructed much more lightly. Although they are described as specially built for rowing, this should probably not be taken to imply that they were without masts and sails. Indeed there seems a direct hint in the Saga that they did indeed have them, for it says that when

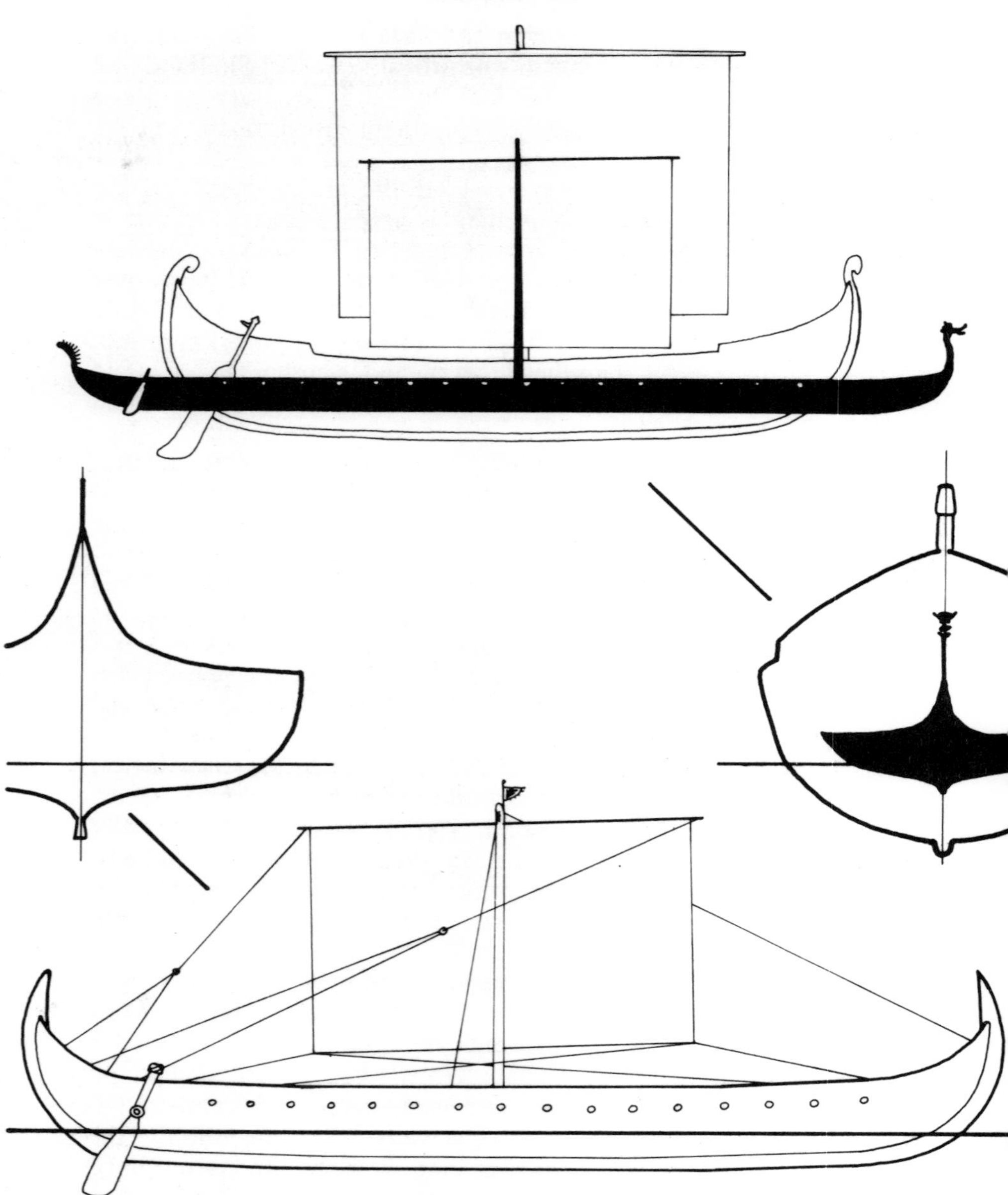

The silhouette of a lightweight rowing warship is superimposed on an oceangoing knarr. Th reconstructions are based on Danish finds at Ladby and Skuldelev.

The Gokstad ship is shown below to the same scales for comparison.

they put to sea from Bergen, they sailed before a favourable breeze.

It is difficult to be sure what size they were. It is not entirely clear whether in saying they were "rather small" the Saga writer was talking in general terms, or specifically in terms of "langskip". By the latter days of the Viking era, to which these vessels belonged, some longships were of considerable size. Even a lesser one, if considered fit for the retinue of an Earl, may have been quite an impressive vessel. The longship recovered from the bed of Roskilde Fjiord at Skuldelev in Denmark appears to have been over ninety feet long, though it may have had as few as 20 pairs of oars (certainly no more than 26). Even the smaller of the fighting craft there, pulling only 12 pairs of oars, was almost sixty feet long, while the warship out of the Ladby grave mound in the same country approached seventy feet in length with apparently only four more pairs of oars. The classic Norwegian grave ships from Oseberg and Gokstad were between seventy and eighty feet long for fifteen and sixteen pairs. It would thus seem not unreasonable to suspect that *Hjolp* and *Fifa* might well fall in the seventy to ninety feet length range.

As specialised rowing vessels, their beam would certainly be narrow. Not enough of the Roskilde longship has survived to be confident of its width, but it seems to have been little more than one seventh of its length. The length:beam ratio of the Ladby ship is about 7.2:1, and when Danish Scouts decided to build a full scale replica they received many warnings that it would prove dangerous. Their copy however was surprisingly seaworthy, swift and lively to handle. As Mr. Ole Crumlin-Pedersen of the Roskilde Museum put it, she rode like a swan on the water, and even transported horses with ease although her maximum beam was just over nine feet.

Unlike the high-sided sailing knarrs, *Hjolp* and *Fifa*, as fast rowing vessels, would have had low freeboard. Their oars probably passed out through ports that could be closed with pivoted covers when not in use. Their draught would be shallow, sacrificing the grip on the water wanted for sailing partly to cut the drag when rowing, and partly to facilitate beaching. The long straight keel would however give good control when running in heavy seas, while the characteristic Viking double-ended form with its marked sheer and generous flare would allow them to keep the seas in any reasonable weather, though clearly they could not compete with knarr and hafskip in really bad conditions.

The seaworthiness of that basic double-ended model in capable hands, is indicated by the way that it remained in use among the Norwegian and Shetland fishermen throughout the days of sail. Men

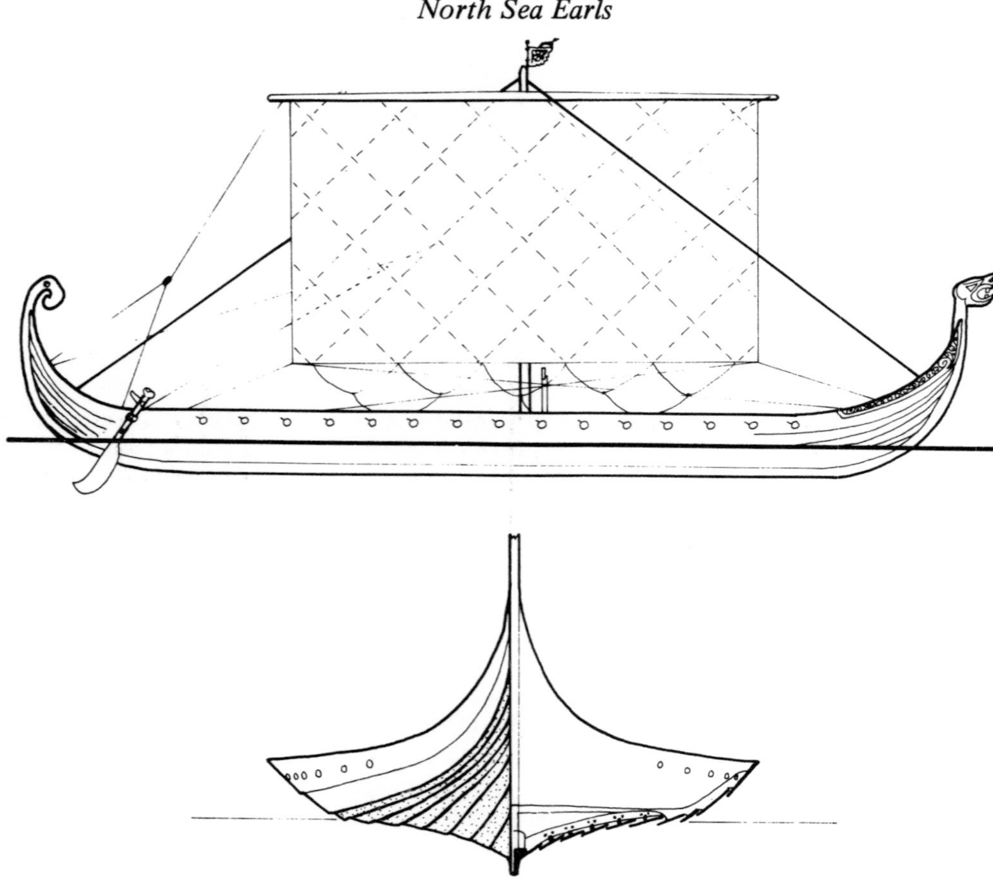

Almost all details are conjectural, but Hjolp *and* Fifa *perhaps looked something like this.*

who have to go offshore in open boats for their living do not lightly change proven designs, and while the resemblance between the particular vessels in which the Earls were wrecked and the small modern Shetland boats is only that between distant members of the same Norse family, when craft of similar sizes and purposes are compared, the relationship can be very close indeed. And we shall see shortly, at Sumburgh the present-day Shetlanders still favour boats that must be very like the one used by Rognvald when he challenged their tide-race there, eight centuries ago.

Let us first, however, complete our appraisal of *Hjolp* and *Fifa.* Some points about them are clearer than others. Thus from archaeological evidence and commonsense considerations of seamanship we can be fairly sure that we are right if we picture the oars that drove these ships so swiftly as having long narrow blades. The broad paddles of Mortlake to Putney catch wind and wave too easily for a seaway, and would hardly fit the metaphor of the oar as the sea's sword that Rognvald used in one of the verses ascribed to the night of the wreck. Again from both material evidence and practical considerations, we may picture the oarsmen set along the side of the ships with their oar ports spaced somewhere between 3 and 3½ feet apart. Strangely enough, however, it is difficult to be sure what they were sitting upon. Some of the recent Viking ship finds have thwarts for their rowers, but the Gokstad and Oseberg ships had no sign of any permanent seating arrangement, and it is generally considered that the oarsmen must have sat on lashed-down sea chests. Perhaps the "great gifts" from Ingi and Rognvald's other kinsmen in Norway were being brought home in just such chests.

Information on the other aspect of the propulsion of the ships is also patchy. If there was as we suspect provision for sailing as well as rowing, we can be sure that this followed the Viking stereotype of a single mast, set just forward of mid-ships, with a single square sail. Since they were primarily rowing vessels, we can be confident that the mast could be lowered to reduce windage while under oars. The ship graves and the wrecks found underwater even give us a very good idea how the mast step would be arranged to allow this. From there on however, puzzles remain. A really complete Viking mast has yet to be found, and there is doubt about how it could be rigged, and even how tall it would be. It is coming to be accepted now that the masts may well have been less tall and the sails wider than the schoolroom image of a Viking ship would suggest. Just what the sails were like and how they were handled is another matter.

Some Gotland picture-stones show sails hung about with astonishing networks of lines. How these worked, and indeed just what they did and whether they were in general use, is still a matter of controversy. On the other hand, it seems quite likely that since *Hjolp* and *Fifa* were gift vessels, the sails themselves may have been decorated. We know that King Haakon Haakonsson's *Mariasuden* had a sail allegedly embroidered with "fair pictures" of some kind a century or so after *Hjolp* and *Fifa*, but this does not seem at all usual. What was common, according to the sagas, was colour-striped sails. The roughly contemporary Bayeux Tapestry shows ships with sails with broad vertical stripes, but sometimes oblique stripes or chequer-boards are believed to have been used. Red and white seem to have been favourite colours. A big pile of yellowish woollen cloth,

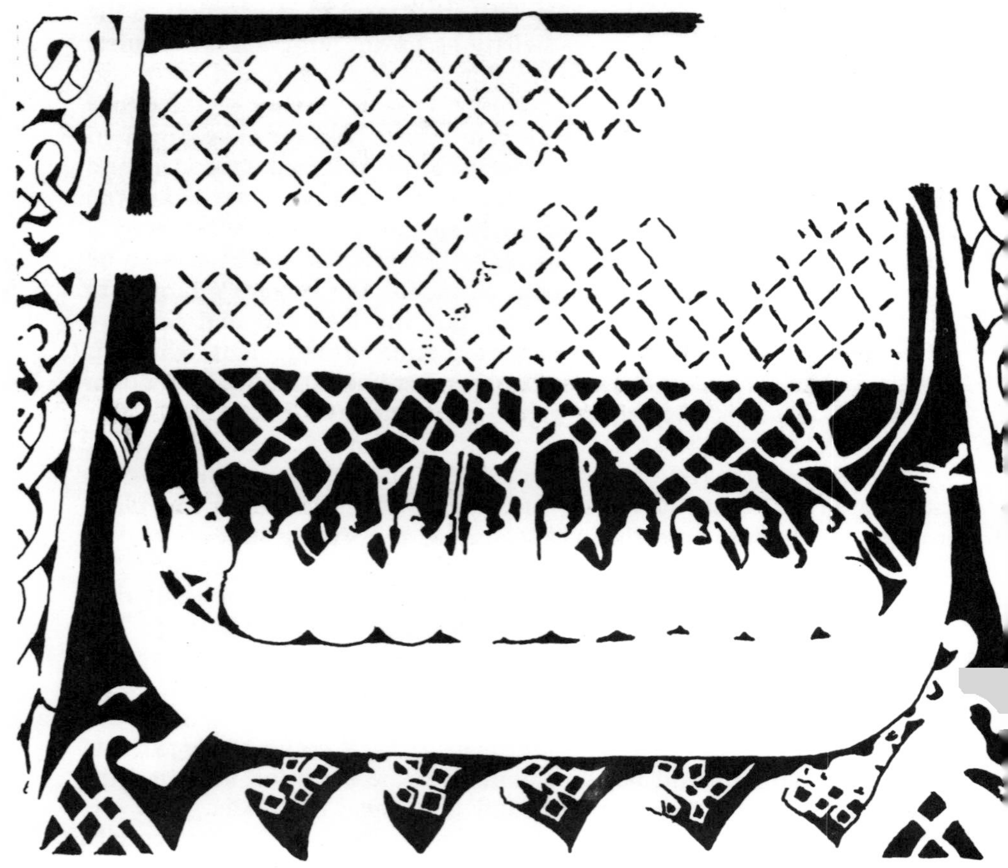

'astonishing networks of lines'

supposedly originally white with red stripes sewn on was found in the bow of the Gokstad ship. This may well have been the sail. Certainly a sail "as white as snow, with stripes of red and blue" is mentioned in the *Saga of St. Olav. Hjolp* and *Fifa* may thus have been quite colourful aloft.

Since they were selected as diplomatic gifts, they may well have had highly ornamental hulls also. We have already got some indication of what this could entail from the description of Limp-Leg's crusading ship for Rognvald. The Saga's account of the decoration of Eindridi's ill-fated dragonship is just as striking. Bow and stern were richly inlaid with gold. The bows were painted,

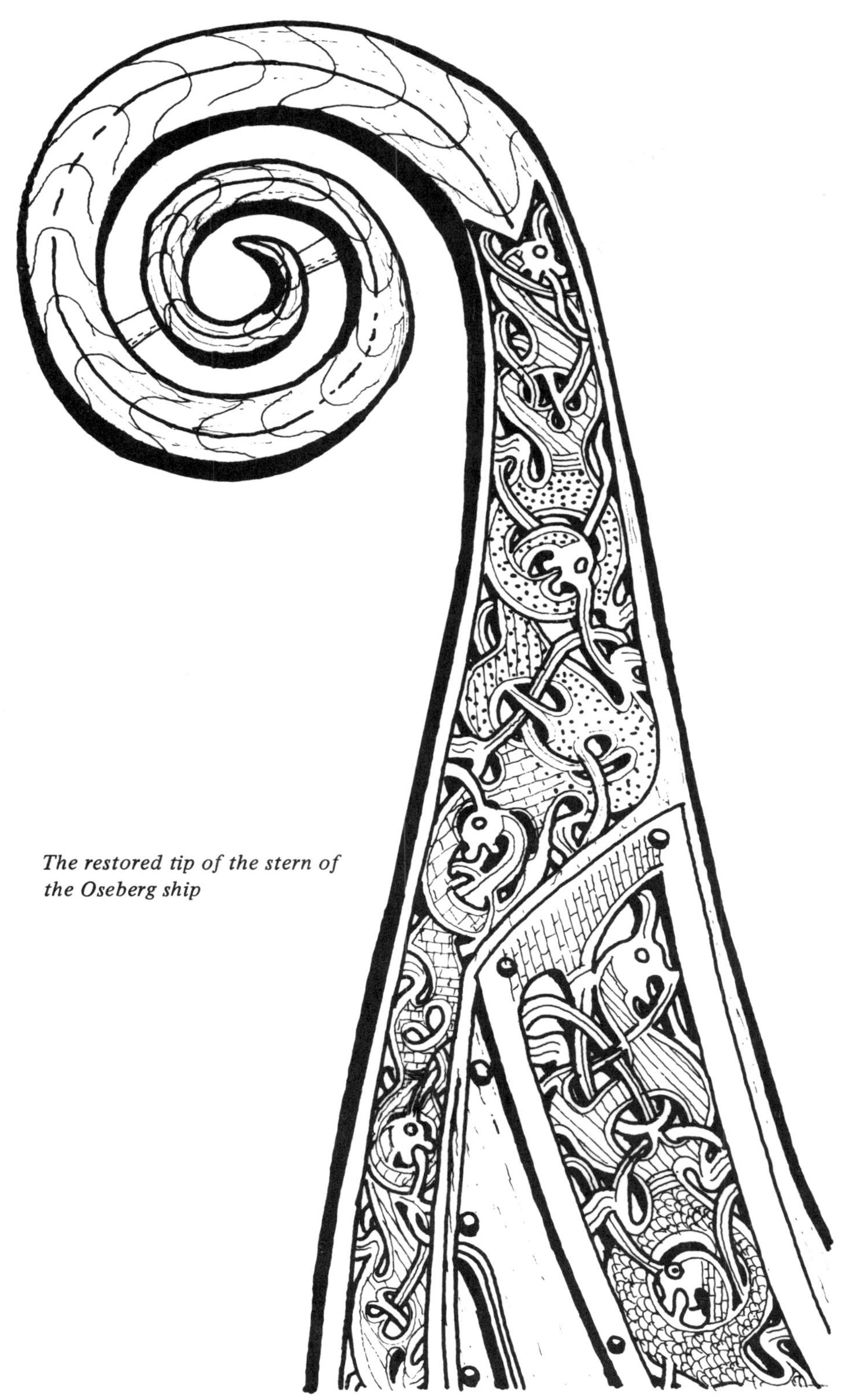

The restored tip of the stern of the Oseberg ship

indeed she was painted all over from gunwale to waterline, wherever it seemed to look well. It will be recalled that Rognvald's ship also had gold inlaid weather vanes, and was not merely painted but carved from stem to stern. The Oseberg ship gives some idea of the kind of effect obtained overall, although the style of the designs reflect its date of circa 800 A.D., i.e. two and a half centuries earlier than *Hjolp* and *Fifa.* It was in that period too that the earliest Norse settlers at Jarlshof in Shetland scratched on stone not only drawings of ships but a close-up of a dragon prow. It seems not unlikely that *Hjolp* and *Fifa* had figureheads, but whether they were dragons is another question.

Dragon's head scratched on a stone at Jarlshof

We are on surer ground when we consider how they were built. From hints spread through the Sagas, and from the evidence of archaeology, we know quite a lot about both the broad design philosophy and the specific "workshop practices" of the Viking

Divers at Stava Geo

Fea Geo – perhaps the site of the wreck of Fifa?

shipwrights. Since we know what they had in mind in building these particular vessels, we can form a very fair idea of how they are likely to have been put together.

As ships designed to be notably fast under oars they must have been very lightly built as well as being long, narrow and slim-lined to slip easily through the water. The structural design problems in this are not altogether unlike those of building a high aspect ratio aircraft wing, and in such cases Viking shipwrights in fact adopted an approach that has much in common with that used by, say, the Boeing engineers in designing the 707's wing. In either case, any fully rigid structure capable of resisting the order of bending stresses involved would be too heavy. A degree of elasticity was the answer for both, and ships and wings with a built-in resilience were therefore evolved. Passengers in modern airliners are often somewhat taken aback when the wings whip visibly. In the same way, when Captain Andersen sailed a replica of the Gokstad ship from Norway to America at the end of last century, his crew were at first very upset to see the gunwales flexing half a foot out of line when heavy seas were encountered. They soon realised however that it was in this resilience that the true strength of the vessel lay.

Besides allowing a light-weight structure, this non-rigid approach has an additional advantage for ships like *Hjolp* and *Fifa*, where speed is of the essence. By showing a little elasticity and not offering dead resistance, a boat with some judicious flexibility in hull and rig tends to come to terms better with wind and wave, to the advantage of its speed. It was well known in the days of the clipper ships that a newly laden vessel would sail like a log until she loosened up and regained her customary suppleness. Dana gives a graphic description of this in *Two Years Before the Mast*. In war it was not unknown for the crew of a pursued vessel not only to jettison cannon but to loosen the mast chocks and even to chop through the reinforcing knees of the hull to gain speed.

This last was a desperate measure. The Vikings built resilience in from the very start, by basing their ships and boats on the shell rather than the skeleton principle. Both systems have advantages, and they have co-existed right up to the present day, through most of the known history of shipbuilding. Superficially, they may look very similar, in that both usually involve keel, ribs and planks. On the skeleton system, however, keel and ribs are erected first, and the resulting fairly rigid framework is then planked over. In this case the skin of the vessel tends primarily to be "waterproofing for the skeleton", and only secondarily structural. This is not so in the other system. Here the vessel is given its essential form and strength by the construction of the shell itself, and ribs are often added retrospectively, and it is their role that is the secondary one.

Skeleton construction: an 18th century ship in frame, before being planked up.

There are various ways of making shells, but the one typical of the Vikings and their descendants in Scandinavia and Shetland is called clinker building. This takes its name from the characteristic method of overlapping the edges of planks and fastening them together along their length by pinning the overlap with nails that are clenched over washers called roves. The vessel takes its shape directly from the form of the planks used. The sides of these are not parallel straight lines, but subtle curves that differ from strake to strake and may indeed be far from parallel on opposite edges of the same plank. The shapes are cunningly harmonised so that as each is bent so that its curve conforms to the free edge of the plank previously set in place, the three dimensional form of the vessel materialises. A mould or temporary bulkhead may be set up amidships to help keep the shape symmetrical, but with small vessels at least, even this is often dispensed with. Fore and aft in the Viking ships the strakes ran into rebates cut in the stem and stern posts. Pre-cut examples of these posts have been found in a bog on the island of Eigg in the Hebrides, where they had apparently been left to season by a local Viking shipwright. His rebates allow not only for the taper of the planks but for the way that they would make the transition from the varying flare of the bow to the curved line of the stem. This is an extraordinarily subtle exercise in three dimensional geometry, yet it was apparently routine to carry it out in advance before the rest of the vessel existed, rather than piece-meal as the planks were fitted. This gives us some hint both of the skill of the individual Viking shipwrights and of the highly evolved state of the tradition within which they worked.

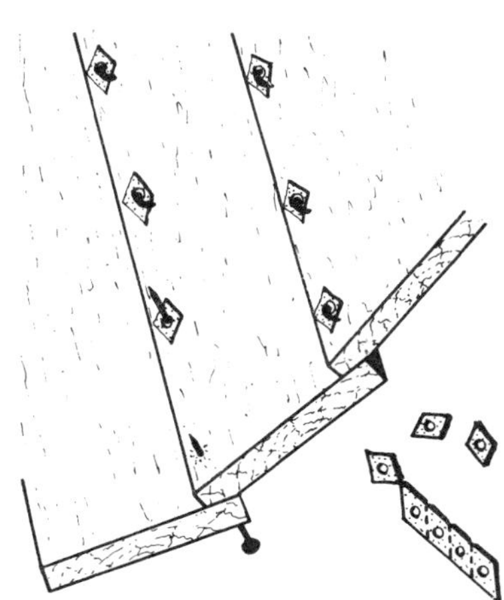

Nails being clenched over roves. Sometimes the point of the nail is simply pinched out, as in riveting, instead of bending it right over.

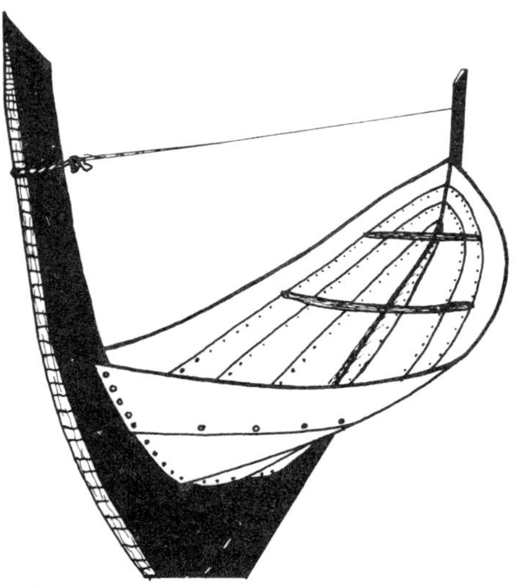

Shell construction: a boat being clinker built. Temporary braces are being used but there are no frames and the form of the hull comes from the shape of the planks themselves.

On the clinker building system, the individual planks used even on quite large vessels could be very thin and flexible indeed. On the eighty foot Gokstad ship, the planks of the main part of the hull were only one inch thick, and we may suspect something of the same order for the vessels of the Earls. The curves imposed on the planks in forming the characteristic Viking flaring hull shape with its marked sheer gave the necessary basic stiffness. When the reinforcing ribs were added, care was therefore taken to do this in such a way that while strength was gained, resilience was not lost.

Examples of shapes to which planks must be cut for clinker building a small boat and longship.

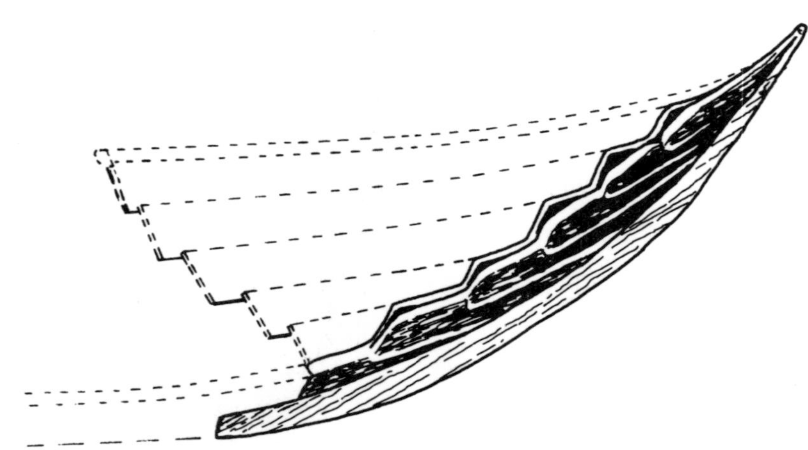

Preformed Viking stem piece from Eigg

This was done in various ways, and several of these can be seen on present day Shetland craft as well as in the Norwegian and Danish Viking ship finds. The ribs are generally small in cross-section, and often they do not run continuously from gunwale to keel, but only link groups of upper or lower strakes. Those crossing the keel, or stem or stern posts, very often arch right over without touching, let alone being attached firmly.

Where the ribs are fixed to the strakes, this is often done with lashings rather than spikes on the Viking vessels. When the planks were dressed, cleats were left standing proud on the inside, to be drilled for the lashings. These were of anything suitably tough, from spruce roots to walrus tendon. If this sounds primitive, think of the subtlety of the problem of choosing the intervals for leaving the

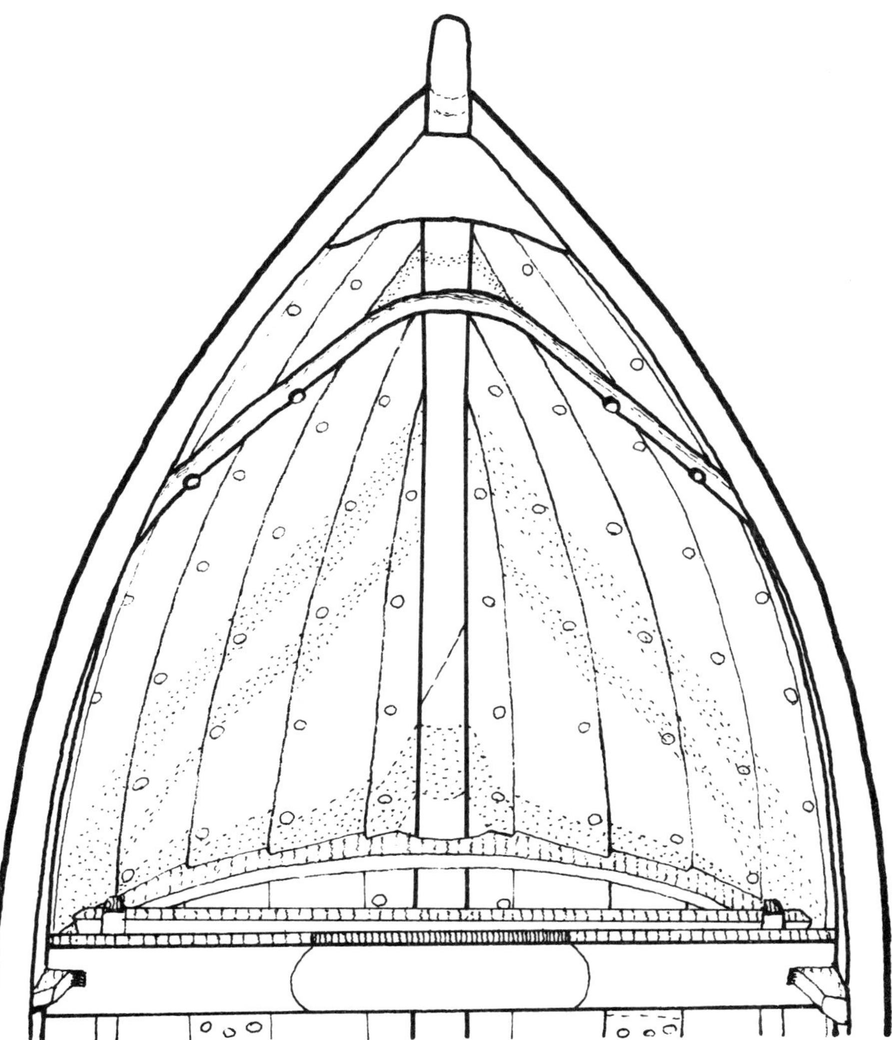

Bow of a Shetland boat, a fourareen. Note the lightness of the cross members, and the way that ribs and stammern arch over the keel without being attached to it.

cleats. The problem had to be solved *before* the timber could be thinned for bending. The spacing had to be varied from plank to plank so that when the flat boards were eventually bent into their complex three dimensional curves in the hull, the cleats would line up in neat vertical rows to accept ribs. It would have been so much easier simply to drive spikes as fixings (as was in fact often done above the waterline where flexibility was less vital). The use of this system of lashing thus gives some measure of the trouble the shipwrights were willing to face to secure the resilience that allowed them to create ship structures that combined strength with light weight.

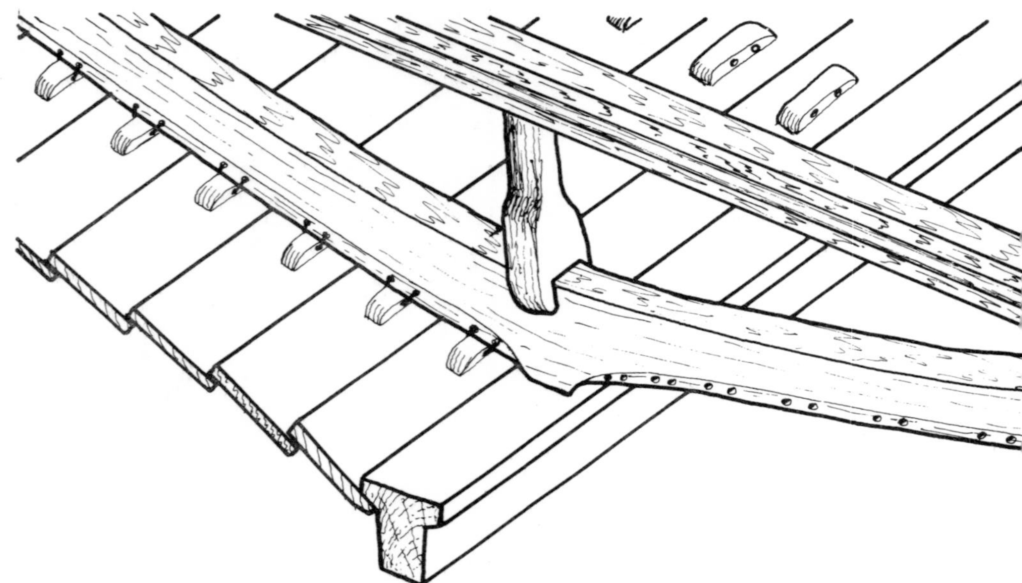

Viking hull construction: the rib is lashed to the cleats on the planks.

Their strength was of a kind designed to resist the dynamic stresses of the seaway but not, however, impact. Thus, while we can envisage *Hjolp* and *Fifa* coping successfully with the strains of the great storm on the Wednesday of the crossing, despite their length and lightness, it is equally easy to understand why there is no mention of salvage attempts after they struck in Shetland. The thin planks and light ribs of those racy vessels are likely to have been quickly reduced to matchwood by the surf that was running that night.

We shall consider the circumstances of their wrecking in the next chapter. Let us first however look a little further at the way that modern and recent Shetland boats show characteristics that would have seemed very familiar to Earl Rognvald or his Norwegian shipbuilder, John Limp-Leg.

As with so many things in Shetland that are rooted in the Viking era, with boats too the Scandinavian link is not merely a relic. Contacts have been maintained down the centuries, right to the present day. Thus when Captain Inkster wanted a fine-lined little boat to teach his boys pulling, it seemed very natural to fetch one home from Norway. Indeed the continuity of contact is particularly noticeable with boat styles, simply because of the absence of trees in Shetland. Rather than merely exporting raw timber, the Norwegians long ago took to building boats on temporary fastenings, then knocking them down again and shipping the components flat for final assembly in Shetland. The notion of do-it-yourself boat kits is nothing new.

This kind of thing may well have been happening in Rognvald's day, and certainly it went on right up to Victorian times. There is a story about the end of the trade, which the reader must assess for himself. It seems that English cabinet-makers successfully lobbied Parliament to put up a tariff barrier. This was really intended to keep out Scandinavian furniture, but it made it very expensive to import any timber products. The special requirements of the Shetland fishermen, six hundred miles to the north of Westminster, had not been kept in mind. This was nothing new. The Lord however helps him who helps himself, so a loophole was found. This was in an addendum secured by a lobby of English brewers which permitted the tax-free import of barrel staves. All went well until a Sooth-Moother customs man took it into his head to investigate why quantities of staves for vast (20 or 30 foot . . .) barrels were being imported through Lerwick. He was not pleased when he found them sailing out to the fishing grounds.

Irrespective of whether Norwegian hands played a direct part in their construction, the Viking lineage of the characteristic Shetland small craft of the present and recent past is clear. Though boats for different purposes vary now as in Viking times in both size and properties, there is no doubt about the family resemblance. The Viking and Shetland models typically are undecked double-ended boats, clinker built with a tendency towards few and rather wide strakes. They are fine lined fore and aft and have a handsome sheer with raking curved stems and low freeboard amidships. They draw little water, and row and beach easily.

The different parts of their boats are known among Shetlanders by names that have an unfamiliar ring to southern ears, and predictably many of these reflect the Norse legacy. The same is true of the terms that were used in fishing and seamanship in general in the days of sail.

Thus, instead of attaching the yard to the mast with a parral, and hoisting it with the halyards, the *rae* is fixed to the *stong* using a *rakki* (often traditionally made from a ram or cow horn) and raised by heaving on the *tows*. In the hull, the reinforcing ribs are *baunds* if they run vertically or *stammerns* where canted at the bow and stern. The planks themselves have special names. Where there are six to a side, from garboard strake to gunwale these are known as the *boddam runner*, the *first* and *second harsings* and *swills*, and the *reebing*. Inboard there may be wooden bars called *fiskabrods* set under the *tafts* (as thwarts are known). These keep a cargo of fish from shifting while letting any sea shipped distribute itself immediately along the length of the boat, so as not to cause bow or stern to plunge. The fish are gaffed and clubbed with a *huggie staff*, and gutted with a *glaun*. If bailing on a really heroic scale is required, the sea is literally shovelled back where it belongs, with a long-handled wooden shovel! At less hectic moments, a wooden hand scoop called an *auskerry* is used. Not only is the name of this Norse, but some seen in use during the Expedition were essentially identical to one found with the Oseberg ship, buried by Vikings three and a half centuries before even Earl Rognvald's time.

The shape of the *auskerry* is an exceedingly practical one for bailing in the corners between garboard and keel, and it is not difficult to see why it has remained in use. The same is true of the system of *kaebs* and *humlabunds* used instead of crutch-type rowlocks or ordinary thole pins. The *kaeb* is the wooden peg against which the oar is pulled, and the *humlabund* is a loose loop that serves two purposes. Besides preventing the waves from jumping the oar over the *kaeb* when rowing, it allows the oarsman instantly to ship his oars, confident in their security however lively the motion of the boat. The modern *kaebs* can be removed so as not to foul nets or lines coming in over the gunwale, and terylene line has replaced walrus or cow hide for the *humlabunds*, but the principle is exactly the same as in Viking rowing boats of the same size range.

This characteristically practical Shetland blend of tradition with innovation comes out not only in the details of the island boats, but in their range of types. Once a good form had been evolved for doing a particular job in particular waters, the proved proportions would be maintained by rigid custom. Build a yole with an extra foot or so on the keel-length compared with what was customary in your district, and the old men might agree she was a bonnie boat, but they would not view her as a true yole. On the other hand, if a change in the economics of the fishing led to a radical change of grounds, sensible new permutations within the overall tradition would be evolved.

This at any rate seems to have been how the best known "Shetland Model" the sixern, arose. The name, sixern, sixareen or sexæring, is derived from the Norse for a six-oared boat, but it has come to be firmly associated with the largest type of Shetland open fishing boat. This was around thirty feet long in its most developed form. These seem to have first emerged as a significant class in the mid-18th century, when the Haaf fishery developed. This was the deep sea as opposed to coastal fishery, when grounds as much as thirty or indeed eventually fifty miles offshore were worked. A vessel with higher freeboard, greater beam and a longer keel in relation to its length was evolved. This gave a good base for working the nets, and more directional stability to reduce the risk of broaching-to when running the long Atlantic seas. Stability and seakindliness were not enough however. Open boats going regularly so far offshore had to be very fast too, so that they could run for it if the weather turned against them. Right up to the end, when the coming of motors rendered them obsolete, the Shetlanders were still seeking to refine the sixern. After the main fishing season closed, boats might even be partially dismantled, and the lines of bow or stern altered by readjusting the clinker planking.

The sixerns are off the sea now, though there is hope that one may be restored and preserved complete. Their form has largely been adopted for the smaller fourareens, however, and these are still very well preserved in Shetland. Indeed, the development of the Shetland model is still continuing. Small versions are built for racing under sail now, and the competition can be fierce.

By no means all the recent smallcraft reflect the sixern's relatively later permutation of the Norse tradition of boatbuilding. Right through, even some of the smallest whillies and eelaboats continued to reflect the old Norway yoles rather than the sixern. Furthermore, the Norse tradition lives on in a remarkably pure form in the Ness yoles. These present day Dunrossness boats are very similar indeed in style and construction to the Viking longboats of comparable size found buried with the Gokstad ship, and also to many of the numerous smallcraft found in the lesser Scandinavian boat burials.

The reasons for this conservatism are thoroughly practical. The modifications of the Norwegian model incorporated in the sixern were evolved to come to terms with the long rollers encountered well out in the ocean. In the coastal waters where the Norwegian and Shetland yoles operated, short lumpy seas are common. In rough weather, reflections of waves from the coast can set up a zone of

The sixern and the smaller Ness Yole

confused cross seas several miles wide, and where the tides of North Sea and Atlantic meet at the extremities of Shetland, the rip currents and races add to the broken water. The Roost of Sumburgh, most marked of these races, is in the area where the Ness yoles operate.

An open boat to survive in such waters must be a lively sea boat, responding fast to the short waves if it is to avoid being swamped. To secure this, in cross section the yoles have a slack bilge and the angle of the garboards tends to be flatter than in the sixern model. They have a strong sheer, with high flared ends to throw the water clear but the minimum safe freeboard elsewhere, to reduce wind resistance. Speed can be crucial to survival amidst the treacherous currents off the headlands. Since the conditions for which the vessels evolved often demanded the use of oars rather than sail, draught is minimal too, to keep down water drag. For good rowing qualities and directional stability, the yole is built slim for its length. A typical one would be between 22 and 23 feet long overall, but with a

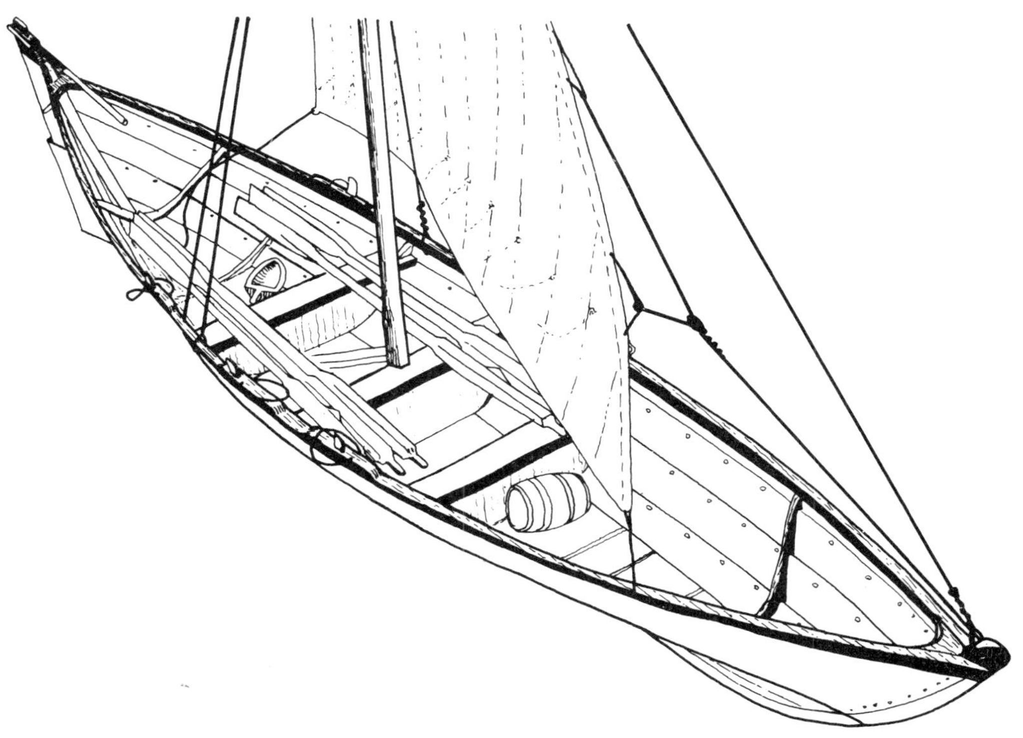

Ness Yole: note the slim lines and minimal structure.

maximum beam of little more than five and a half feet. The men sit in tandem, each pulling a pair of oars. Their thwarts are only three feet apart, concentrating the crew's weight amidships to enhance the boat's lively response to steep seas. When the high aspect ratio and low all-up weight (of only perhaps half a ton) is combined with three determined men pulling six ten foot oars, these are potent craft indeed.

The light weight is attained by a classical application of the principle of resilience discussed earlier. This is to be seen in differing degrees in all the Shetland boat types, and even in the heavier sixern it was standard practice for the sailsman to keep the sole of his foot on the garboard strake to feel from the extent it was quivering whether the boat was being over-driven. All the same, it was not unknown for the thin planks to split in the bows when beating hard to windward. The sixerns were reinforced against this, but in some at least of the lighter Shetland yoles, as in some of the smaller Norwegian craft, the opposite stratagem was employed. In their cases, the resistance of the bows to pounding was enhanced not by stiffening them but by increasing their elasticity. The wales that

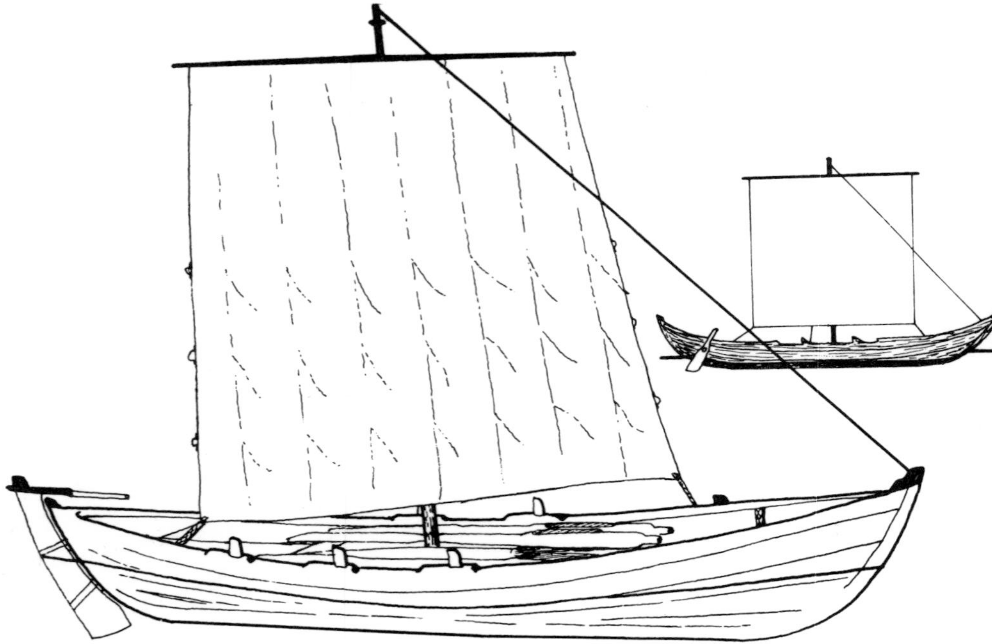

Squaresails on 20th century Fair Isle and 9th century Gokstad boats.

strengthen the boats longitudinally were tapered away finely (so as not to localise stresses) and ended completely one or two feet from the stem and stern posts. As might be expected from this, the internal structure of the yoles is minimal. There are only two major ribs in a two man boat, or three in a three man, and as is typical in Shetland and Viking small craft, these arch over the keel instead of being attached firmly to it. The stammerns do the same over the stem and stern posts.

The rig of the Ness yole is hardly seen these days, but traditionally it consists of a lugsail, cut very flat in the head and very reminiscent of the Viking square-sail carried by the little Gokstad longboat. The skiffs of nearby Fair Isle retained their square-sails into the present century.

All in all, then, it seems that in form, construction and handling, the boats to be seen around Dunrossness today must indeed be very similar to the craft in which Earl Rognvald found himself rowing against the tide-race there, soon after his shipwreck. Before following him to Sumburgh, however, let us first see what more can be learned of the fate of *Hjolp* and *Fifa*.

Chapter 4

Shipwreck and Saga

The first thing that the Expedition needed to do in Shetland was to try to find out how far the account of the wrecking of the Earls given in *Orkneyinga Saga* ought to be viewed as fact or fiction. There seemed no good reason to doubt that Harald and Rognvald had in fact been wrecked in Shetland on their return from the court of King Ingi. There was no guarantee however that the Saga writer, working sometime after the event and probably living in Iceland, had not invented details wholesale. It will be remembered that his concern was not primarily to record the accidental demise of the two vessels. Though swift and handsome, they counted only as minor warships. His aim was rather to use the incident as a vehicle for developing the image of Rognvald that he wished to communicate. It was therefore quite possible that if details had not come to him, he would have made them up to give the event vividness for his readers. Indeed he might even have taken over some account of a quite different shipwreck that seemed readymade to fit his purpose, just as the writer of *Egil's Saga* seems in turn to have pirated this part of *Orkneyinga Saga* for his account of Egil's shipwreck in England. It was thus very necessary for the Expedition to look hard at the Saga account and try to judge whether it was compatible with the part of the Shetland coastline to which it was ascribed. Only if this seemed to be so would it be worth trying to use the details of the account to try to identify areas for underwater searches. This chapter therefore deals primarily with the overall veracity of the Saga.

Let us then look at what the text says, and at how far this matches with what the Expedition found out about the conditions characteristic of the area.

Orkneyinga Saga tells us that it was a Tuesday evening when the Earls put to sea. They may have left at that time of day with the intention of pacing their trip so that they had a fair chance of approaching Orkney sometime in daylight hours, a couple of days later, without having to lie-to at sea off an unlit coast. Alternatively, it may simply be that it was in the evening that they got a favourable wind. At any rate, at first all went well. They cleared the Norwegian coast and spent the night sailing before a good breeze. As we saw in the last chapter, the implication appears to be that they were actually under sail, not under oars.

The wind began to rise, however, and Wednesday was very stormy. The Saga says no more than this, but from what we have seen of the likely form of *Hjolp* and *Fifa* in the last chapter, we can guess that they had their hands full. With the previous night's good run behind them, they were well clear of any shelter from the Norwegian coast and the low freeboard of the longships must have made them very vulnerable to the sort of lumpy seas that can blow up quickly in those waters. They would have had to keep end-on to the waves, for the dangers of broaching-to were considerable. Not only were the bulwarks low, but these were essentially open boats and probably heavily laden for their size, what with the retinue of the Earls, their goods and gifts. It would be only too easy to swamp such a vessel in a seaway, and one can well imagine watchful eyes peering to windward through the spindrift, and the most skilled men taking turns at the steering oar.

Whether they ran before the storm under a rag of sail or lay-to with a few oars out, we can not be sure. Perhaps the latter is more likely since the Saga shows that they managed to keep together. With light vessels in stress of weather it can be very difficult indeed to match speeds under sail. With only a single square sail to adjust each, the problem would be even greater than with more modern rigs, unless the strange systems of lines seen on the picture stones mentioned in the last chapter represent an even more ingenious system of sail control than we have yet realised. It is probably more reasonable to envisage them nosing into the storm, with enough oars out forward to give them steerage way and to maintain contact by matching the rates at which they made leeway. If so, their masts would be lowered, to reduce wind resistance and stop them rolling and working so heavily. Nevertheless, their light planks and ribs would be anything but dead to the sea's motion, and their gunwales would flex visibly, as Captain Anderson found with his Gokstad replica.

The Saga tells us nothing directly about the next day, Thursday, but from the circumstances of the wreck that night, with heavy breakers on the Shetland coast, we can deduce that offshore a heavy swell must have been running, though from the way that the text associates the great storm specifically with Wednesday, it seems reasonable to presume that the strength of the wind had gone down somewhat on Thursday. Sometime, too, as the storm went through, the wind direction seems to have veered. It must have been from somewhere out of the east when they sailed before it, as the Saga describes, in their first night's fair run out of Bergen. For them to fetch up unintentionally in Shetland while aiming for Orkney, the wind would seem to have gone further into the south without their realising it. This is not difficult to envisage. Like Sandy Sutherland, on his unexpected visit to the Finn-wyfe, they had no compass. There is little evidence of the magnetic compass being in common use in northern waters for another century. If the windshift occurred during overcast conditions when neither sun nor stars were visible, as was very likely in those days of storm, it is hardly surprising that they failed to detect it and got set north of their course.

It would seem then that the situation aboard *Hjolp* and *Fifa* as they moved through the darkness of Thursday night may have been as follows. The crew were entering their third night afloat in open boats. Few are likely to have had much sleep, certainly since Tuesday. None would have had hot food since Bergen, and all would be tired by the struggle against the storm. Even the lively motion of boats of that type in a seaway would be exhausting, and during the storm some of each crew may also have spent hours pulling long sweeps in rough water. The vessels were still together, though the Saga makes it clear that it was extremely dark, so presumably they were using lanterns to keep station. The incident of Asa falling into the well "in the fog" suggests that the night may have been misty at sea too. If there was fog this may have deadened the sound of the breakers until they were virtually upon them. In any case, however,

Eric Dobbie of Tyneside B.S.A.C.

Denis Mott tries the flux-gate magnetometer on the King's Knowe

The long slab in the top of the King's Knowe, with dark Trebister Ness in alignment with the Bard o'Bressay sunlit beyond

the alertness of the tired crews was probably not great. They had probably relaxed after having successfully weathered the worst of the storm the day before, for they certainly do not seem to have realised that they were so near to land.

The account that the Saga gives of the circumstances of the wreck itself, as opposed to Rognvald's reactions to it, is bald indeed. It says simply that during the Thursday night they sighted land; it was very dark; they could see surf of breakers all round them; up to then they had kept company; now there was no choice but to run both ships ashore; and so they did. Shades of meaning in the next passage will have to be discussed further in the next chapter, but for the moment it can be paraphrased as follows: There was a stony beach in front of them, a narrow strip of shore, and cliffs beyond. The Saga then goes on to tell that all the men survived, though they lost many goods (some of which washed ashore in the course of the night).

The focus shifts then to Rognvald's reactions, and as noted in Chapter 1, the Saga writer is particularly keen to demonstrate his nerve and indeed panache under stress, by quoting verses that he is alleged to have made up on the spur of the moment, literally while still fresh from the autumn sea. These "Scaldic" verses, typical of a class of highly formalised Norse poetry, are more impressive for their tortuous though delightful metaphors than for adding information to our picture of the events of that night. We saw in the last chapter that he referred to an oar as a sea sword; in fact that was only incidental to a reference to his fingers as "sea's sword's hollow places" in a verse in which his arm is "the hawk's bridge" and poetry itself is "Grimnir's (or Odin's) drink". Metaphors from seamanship, falconry and mythology intermingle.

Two of the verses introduce useful fragments however. Once ashore, Rognvald was soon taken in at a farm, and the lady of the house brought him a skin cloak, apparently none too new. He took this with some amusement, clearly thinking of the finery abandoned so recently to the sea. Lucy Collings translated this verse thus for the Expedition:

"I shake a wrinkled skin – it is small ornament for me – whenever we may go splendidly adorned from the wet eel's field's steed[1] ; the ship-field[2] is deep, where it stands over our outer garments; the breakers drove the horse of Hunn[3] against the cliffs". ([1] ship; [2] sea; [3] ship).

Just how literally should the reference to driving against the cliffs be taken, and how does this square with the stony beach of the Saga writer? If there appears to be conflict between the verse and the matrix in which it is embedded in the Saga, how should one judge between them? The poem may not actually have sprung from Rognvald while he was still damp with brine, but it is nevertheless firmly attributed to him and there are many precedents for earlier poetic fragments being incorporated in Sagas. If it is genuine, it has two advantages. Firstly, Rognvald, unlike the Saga writer, was a participant in the event, and was versifying for contemporaries some of whom at least would be fully conversant with the circumstances. Secondly, the highly convoluted style of his formal utterances hardly lends itself to casual reworking: those of his verses that survived at all were quite likely to be handed down unmodified, as entire artefacts. Against this, however, was the constraint of brevity, that may well have led him to use an approximation rather than a fully accurate factual statement, simply because it seemed to him to fit more satisfactorily into the type of poetic statement he had in mind. Nevertheless, if the verse is indeed by Rognvald, it is unlikely that he as a participant would include something entirely misleading, and any approximation would probably relate fairly closely to what actually happened.

In the other case that yields information, it is not the content of the verse itself but its introduction that is important. There are again problems of evaluation, but in this case, the piece of information is the key one that gives a direct clue to the part of Shetland in which the shipwrecks took place. Without this, it would have been impossible to bring fieldwork and diving research techniques to bear on the problem of the Saga writer's veracity, and the debate would have remained in the literally and figuratively drier context of the university libraries at Cornell and Edinburgh.

The verse in question contains only Rognvald's remarks on a proud and unco-operative farmer. When the crews had got ashore, they soon found farms where they were taken in. It is unlikely that there were less than fifty of them, and with the Earl's retinues there may well have been something nearer twice that number between the two ships. With farmsteads not unlike the crofts of recent generations (cf. Chapters 2 and 6), the shipwrecked sailors could not be sheltered under any one roof but would have to spread themselves between the farms of the district. The Saga confirms that they did this. Furthermore it says that when Rognvald sent a dozen of his men to one Einar, the reply was that he would not take them in unless the Earl came himself. This was the occasion of Rognvald's scathing verse.

The important thing is that the Saga says specifically that the Earl sent his men to Einar *at Gulberuvik*: "Jarl sendi menn sína tólf til Einars á Gullberuvik". The degree of survival of Norse placenames in Shetland has already been noted in Chapter 2. There seems little doubt among Scandinavian, British and American scholars that this placename has survived as Gulberwick, and that it places the shipwrecks in the general area of the bay of that name, immediately south of Lerwick on the east side of the mainland of Shetland.

Note that the conclusion was that it was in that general area. Of itself, the statement in the Saga does not necessarily imply that the ships were lost within that bay. Indeed, if the placename is read as referring to the bay as a feature (and – vík means bay or inlet), the sentence would seem to suggest that Rognvald was elsewhere with his men. On that reading it would be reasonable to conclude that the wrecks did not take place in Gulberwick but nearer to the farm where the Earl had set up his headquarters. Wherever that was, however, it is unlikely to have been far from Gulberwick for him to send survivors there.

It seems not unlikely however that the common practice of naming one of the larger or earlier established farmsteads on an inlet by the name of that inlet was in use there too. If Gulberuvik referred to a farmstead of that name belonging to Einar somewhere around the bay now called Gulberwick, then the scene of the wrecking might very well have been that bay itself, with Rognvald merely sending the dozen men round its shores from whatever farm he himself had adopted as his headquarters. This reading gains support from the fact that there is an old farm above the head of the bay, now abandoned, called Wick. The Scandinavian scholar, Finnbogi Gudmundsson, suggests that this is a simple contraction of Gulberwick/Gulberuvik. That steading is set well back from the sea. Other modern farms, and traces of platforms on the slopes where earlier ones have stood, lie considerably closer to the shores of the bay. If the identification of Wick with the site of Einar's steading is correct (and other farms by the bay, such as Setter, have kept names that go back even further into Norse times), then its extra distance from the sea might well explain why Rognvald only appears to have sent men there towards the end of the wreck episode (if the order of the passages in the Saga is meaningful).

Many present day Shetlanders and several Victorian and Edwardian books originating in Shetland were confident that the wrecks had indeed taken place in Gulberwick itself. Lucy Collings carefully followed up the slim possibility that this local certainty might reflect a survival of oral tradition concerning the wrecks. The

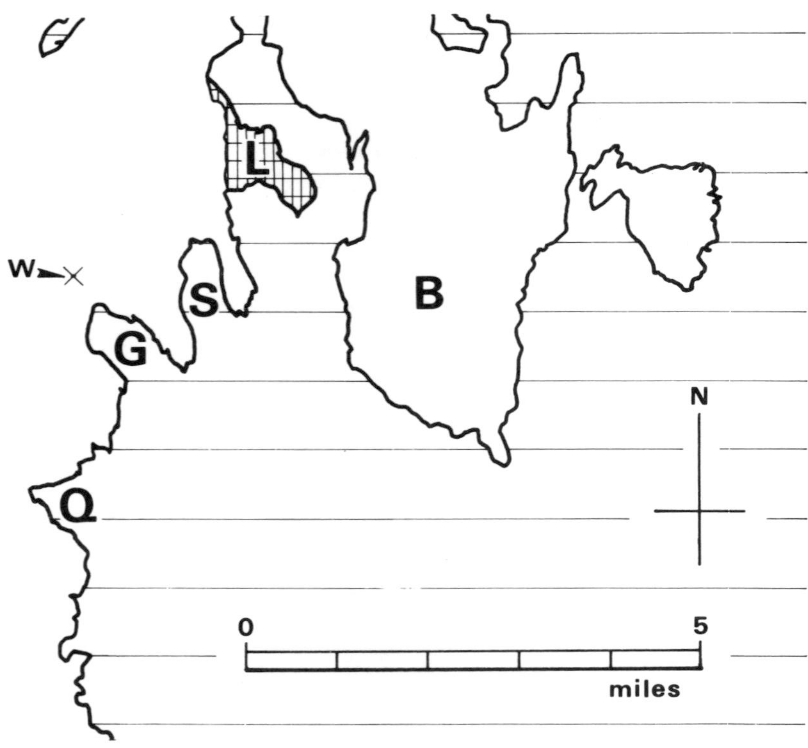

L. Lerwick   B. Bressay   S. Voe of Sound   G. Gulberwick   Q. East Voe of Quarff   W. Wick farm

speedy location of the Armada ship, *el Gran Grifon*, on Fair Isle and of several other shipwrecks in Shetland has owed much to the accuracy of local traditions. The Vikings however lie twice as far back into the past as the Armada, and the very popularity of the Sagas and Viking-lore in general in modern Shetland made it very difficult to detect anything but feedback from the printed page. Memories seemed to have been influenced too by the first Up Helly Aa to take place after the Second World War. In this a Gulberwick man, the scholarly Laurence Johnson, was Guizerjarl and took the part of Earl Rognvald, and the Gulberwick tradition of the landing was reinforced. Unfortunately with the amalgamation or abandonment of many of the old crofts around the bay in the earlier part of this century, there was a considerable turnover of population, and almost all the families now living there are from other parts of Shetland. They were generous in their help to the Expedition, and while not claiming to be repositories of the old traditions of the area they gave valuable firsthand information on the special characteristics of local sea conditions. This certainly helped in reconstructing what conditions were likely to have been like in the area in Viking times.

Let us now examine this, without for the moment going any further in pursuit of the specific sites of the wrecks than the working hypothesis that these may have taken place either at the bay of Gulberwick itself or within easy reach of it.

The first priority is to get some impression of the extent to which the basic form of the coast may have changed since Viking times. Gulberwick is flanked by two other bays. To the south is the East Voe of Quarff, while to the north the Voe of Sound intervenes between Gulberwick and Lerwick. On one of the readings of the Saga proposed above, any of this area might be relevant. However, it was clearly not going to be possible to search all of it underwater with the resources available to the Expedition. Since as we have seen there was no prospect of coming across anything as easily identifiable as cannon, say, a very intensive type of diver search would be required. Rather than dissipate resources in many widely scattered small search areas, a decision was taken early in the Expedition to concentrate on one bay, so that a substantial proportion of the more promising areas there might be covered. Since the second reading favoured Gulberwick itself (and also possibly because a lot of Shetlanders would have thought us quite mad if we had *not* looked there!) this was given priority. The work on the extent of post-Viking coastal change was therefore also concentrated there, though much of it was also applicable to the two neighbouring Voes, where the range of landforms is not dissimilar.

The area was first studied using stereoscopic aerial photographs, and coastal details were transferred from these onto a base map drawn at a scale of 1:2500 (i.e. about 25 inches to the mile). Data were also compiled from large scale maps recently completed by the Ordnance Survey, and from the Admiralty Chart. The mapping of the cliff and beach features was then checked in detail on the ground.

During the course of this work several possible archaeological sites were spotted on the air photographs. These were also followed up and either eliminated or recorded in the field. Others not visible in the photographs were found too, particularly when investigating the open sections under the tops of the cliffs. Most exciting was a previously unrecorded fortification on a cliff promontory, and Drs.

Duncan McArdle and Ian Morrison made a detailed survey of this.

To start the underwater work, the Expedition advance party made a fast but systematic reconnaissance of the shallower parts of Gulberwick by snorkelling. That is, they kitted up in most of their diving gear but left the aqualungs themselves behind, and dived simply by holding their breath. Travelling light in this way, they could swim and plunge quickly, rapidly building up an impression of the bottom characteristics of the area. The girls of the shore party co-ordinated the operation, and using sextants, conned the swimmers seawards along parallel grid lines set at 100 metre intervals along the shores of the bay. On each line, a pair of snorkellers swam out, duck-diving until they either encountered unbroken sandy bottom with nothing to report, or reached their personal depth limit. Not many cigarette smokers were reporting from the fifty foot mark . . . They then swam inwards, checking and identifying points where there were well defined changes in bottom topography. At these points they stopped and signalled to the shore party who fixed their position by optical rangefinder. On reaching the shore at the end of each leg, without leaving the water they gave a description of the different segments they had just indicated. This was written down by the girls on the rocks, and plotted directly on the field copy of the base map. They then swam along a hundred metres, and set off along the next transect.

At one point, the rangefinder operator was puzzled to find that even allowing for the double images given by the device, she had too many little glossy black heads bobbing in her field of view. She brought the images of the furthest diver into coincidence, and realised that the reason that he was not using a snorkel like the others was that he was a seal .. apparently much intrigued by the strange goings on in his bay.

As the Expedition proceeded, the geomorphological questions about the recent evolution of the bay posed by this reconnaissance were followed up by Ian Morrison. The deeper areas were explored with aqualungs until all the various landform units represented in and around the bay had been sampled. A quantitative picture of the submarine morphology was then obtained by using a paper-recording echo sounder. With this, a lattice of cross and longitudinal profiles of the bay was measured, running along lines selected as characteristic on the basis of the snorkelling and aqualung diving reconnaissances.

This was done using one of the Expedition's inflatable diving boats. Normally, paper recorders and electronics do not take happily to wet trips in these "galloping black puddings" (as one of the

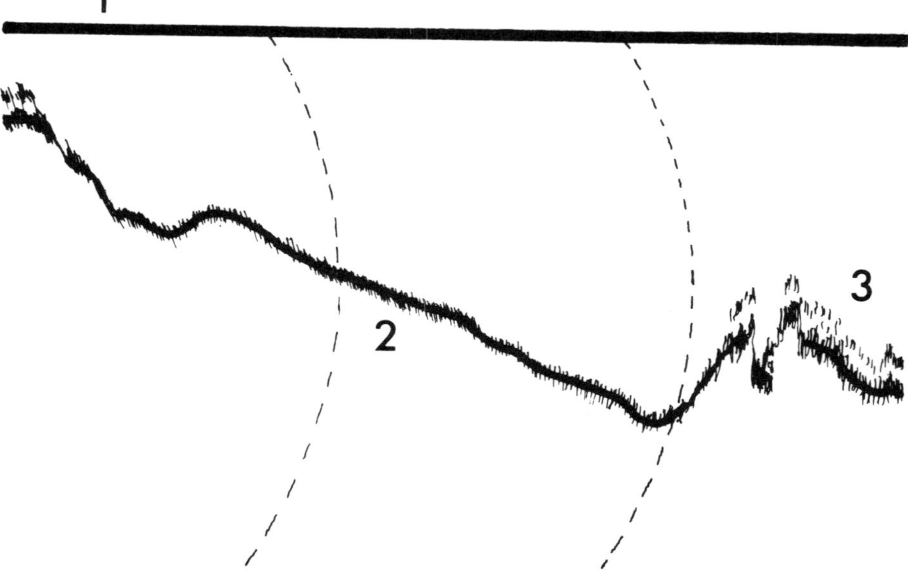

Echo sounder trace:
1: Surface 2: Sandy bottom 3: Kelp on rock

Tyneside divers was heard to describe them). This particular echo-sounder belonged to the Slough divers however, and they had built a waterproof casing for it. This was just as well. One morning, only one run was needed to complete a set of profiles. This traverse lay down the length of the bay and out of its mouth. Though there was some sea running, conditions offered no real problems. We started the run at the bay-head beach, and began the long haul out towards Trebister Ness. The boat was kept on course by looking out aft, and keeping the gable of the little Gulberwick church lined up in transit with a particular point on the hill above. The blunt nose of the "black pudding" began to biff into the lumpy seas rolling up the bay, and showers of spray burst aboard. This did not trouble those of us dressed in wet-suits, but one of the team, an RAF survival instructor, was dressed for another of the day's jobs. Since he was wearing an ordinary polo neck jersey and cloth trousers, he crouched down with his back to the low dodger in the bows, his knees about his ears. He was also wearing thigh waders, and this posture proved his undoing. Unfortunately, at the very moment we ran out from under the shelter of the Ness, our coxswain injudciously chose to look sternwards to check his course by the church transit. The nose of the boat smacked hard into the first big sea, and the top of the wave came over the bow in a lump. The echo-sounder, though jarred, remained dry within its case. But the tops of the waders, pointing forward like scoops over the ducked head of their wearer, snatched into the boots a quantity of water that seemed to run into gallons rather than mere pints. A sad voice said, "Now we know why they're called *sea* boots . . . "

When there was any doubt about the nature of the features shown up by the echo-sounder trace, this was checked by direct observation on further dives. In this way, bedrock ridges and platforms, unlikely to have changed much in the geologically-short space of time since the Viking period, were distinguished with certainty from possibly evanescent landforms of sand or shingle.

As will be shown in the next chapter, signs were found that certain areas and features had changed since Viking times. On the whole however, both the general layout of coast and seabed, and the range of landforms present, did seem thoroughly compatible with the account given in *Orkneyinga Saga* of the wrecking of the Earls.

Let us look first at the overall pattern of the coast. Both Gulberwick and the Voe of Sound open to the south-east, and when there is a northward set, the headlands that protrude to the north of each bay tend to send surface currents curling into them. This tendency is particularly marked in the case of Trebister Ness with Gulberwick. As we have seen, the Earls had certainly been set well to the north of their intended course. Had the implication of the Saga instead been that they had drifted southward, say, this would have made any hypothetical entrance to the Voe of Sound, Gulberwick or even the East Voe of Quarff much more difficult to envisage because of the barriers offered in that case by the Nesses and the big island of Bressay beyond.

Secondly, the layout of the seabed itself seemed to fit well with what the Saga said. This was true of all three bays to some extent, but again Gulberwick offered the most striking case. Ian Morrison concluded from the geomorphological survey that at certain wave frequencies, the way the bay shoals within the Nesses of Setter and Trebister might well cause broken water to occur *inside* the bay when there was only a heavy swell on the deeper waters outside. This, taken together with the darkness and probable mistiness of the night, would certainly explain the crews suddenly finding breakers all round them. This point was checked carefully with people who lived and fished around Gulberwick. They, and Captain Inkster the Lerwick harbourmaster (who used to have a cottage on the bay) confirmed that it was in fact so, and that it is indeed not uncommon for the whole surface of Gulberwick to be breaking when there is only an oily swell outside. Even when surf is not general, waves often break on the Kirk Bar in the centre of the bay. This is a bedrock reef, and was certainly at least as much in evidence in Viking times. The Saga thus seems to be thoroughly compatible with the special conditions of the Gulberwick area.

Thirdly, it will be recalled that when the Saga writer describes the circumstances of the landing he mentions the accumulations of boulders and shingle in assocation with cliffs or at least steep sea slopes. The wording of the original is rather ambiguous (to modern eyes at least) and the exact relationship of these elements is not altogether clear. They are however plentifully represented today in the piece of coast under investigation, in the whole gamut of possible relations, and there is every indication that this was just as likely in geological terms a thousand years ago.

All in all then, there seems nothing in the Saga account of the wrecking that rings false in terms of the part of Shetland to which it is ascribed, and much that rings true. If the Saga writer invented the details, or pirated material from a description of some other wrecking in some source now lost, then he must have been very lucky indeed in what he put in and what he left out. In some of the Sagas, the time gap between the events described and the period of composition is a long one. The voyage of the Earls took place late in the Viking era, however, and internal evidence on the date of the Saga suggests that parts may have taken shape while men alive at the time of the shipwreck still lived. It is not clear that the composer of the Saga himself knew Shetland, but although an Icelandic background is often evident, he clearly was not unfamiliar with Orkney and parts of Caithness. Rognvald's faction had strong links with both these areas, so the writer might easily enough have heard accurate accounts of the events of that night. The work of the Expedition certainly seems to support the view that his version of them reads more like fact than fiction.

Chapter 5

Diver Search

As soon as it became clear that it was reasonable to place some weight on the Saga account of the wrecking of the Earls, the diver search for actual traces of the event could get under way. As we have seen, the whole area around Gulberwick, including the Voe of Sound and the East Voe of Quarff, might be relevant but it was impracticable to subject all of this to the kind of really intensive underwater search that seemed mandatory.

An operational decision was necessary, and the Expedition's choice of concentrating on Gulberwick itself was ultimately made on a variety of grounds. Gudmundsson's reading of Gulberuvik as indicating farmstead rather than bay was one. Another was the Saga description of the crews suddenly finding breakers all round them, and having to run themselves ashore. This seemed to fit embayment in Gulberwick or the Voe of Sound better than in the more open bay at Quarff. Then, because of the relationship of the two more northerly bays to Bressay, it seemed easier to envisage that vessels coming blindly from somewhere to the eastwards might fetch up in Gulberwick rather than in the Voe of Sound. Finally, it was felt that despite the problems in assessing whether any elements of genuine oral tradition lurked beneath the overlay of modern speculation, it would be foolish altogether to disregard local opinion.

Having decided to put most of its eggs in the Gulberwick basket, the Expedition next had to decide where in that bay it should, or indeed could, concentrate its efforts. Since the work would have to be so labour-intensive, even with the large and keen team available, it was clearly going to be impossible to search every bedrock crevice, sand body or boulder spread in a bay a mile and a quarter long and over half a mile in breadth.

In some stretches of the coastline it was obvious that the landforms had never been compatible with the Saga, and these areas could thus be safely left out of the search programme. Less happily, other parts of the bay that seemed likely areas for shipwreck in the conditions implied by the Saga, exhibited characteristics that almost entirely precluded the survival of artefacts on the seabed. If the ships fetched up there, there would now seem to be virtually no chance of securing direct evidence of the fact. In several other very likely areas, effective search was impracticable with the available resources because of the sheer tonnage of loose rock or shifting sand that would have had to have been excavated and sifted.

The kind of area that could be considered incompatible with the Saga includes much of the coast towards Trebister Ness, seaward of Stava Geo. Vertical cliffs often rise directly from deep water there, and there appears to be no geological reason for envisaging a different situation in Viking times. The Saga states specifically that the complete crews of both vessels survived the wreck, and suggests that they ran the ships ashore while still retaining some measure of control at least. It is very difficult indeed to conceive how every one of the considerable number of men involved could have survived if they had had to contrive to get out of the breakers there and scale those crags in the dark. Rognvald's verse certainly says that the breakers drove the ship (his "horse of Húnn") against the cliffs. In that situation, if they did retain any control at all, they would surely have tried at least to claw along until there was some sign of a foot-hold at water level.

If that was the kind of thing that happened, they might well have ended up in Stava Geo, as in the cod end of a trawl. There boulder accumulations occur, part landslide and part beach. These would certainly fit with one interpretation of the slightly problematic passage about stony material at the landing spot, mentioned in the last chapter. The key word in the Saga is *udr*, and Lucy Collings and

Bob Farrell found that the range of meaning for this centres round a heap of broken stones, with usage applying it to the result of a landslip as well as to stony beach features. The word Geo means a very narrow cliffed inlet, and though this is just what Stava Geo is like, there is a grass slope at the back. This is steep, but while scrambling up is awkward, it is not dangerous. The geological structure at the Geo is such as to suggest that while the cliffs are currently being freshened up by the sea, both their basic layout and the probability of there being an equivalent boulder beach and grassed slope was much the same in Viking times as now. Stava Geo was therefore selected as a major search area.

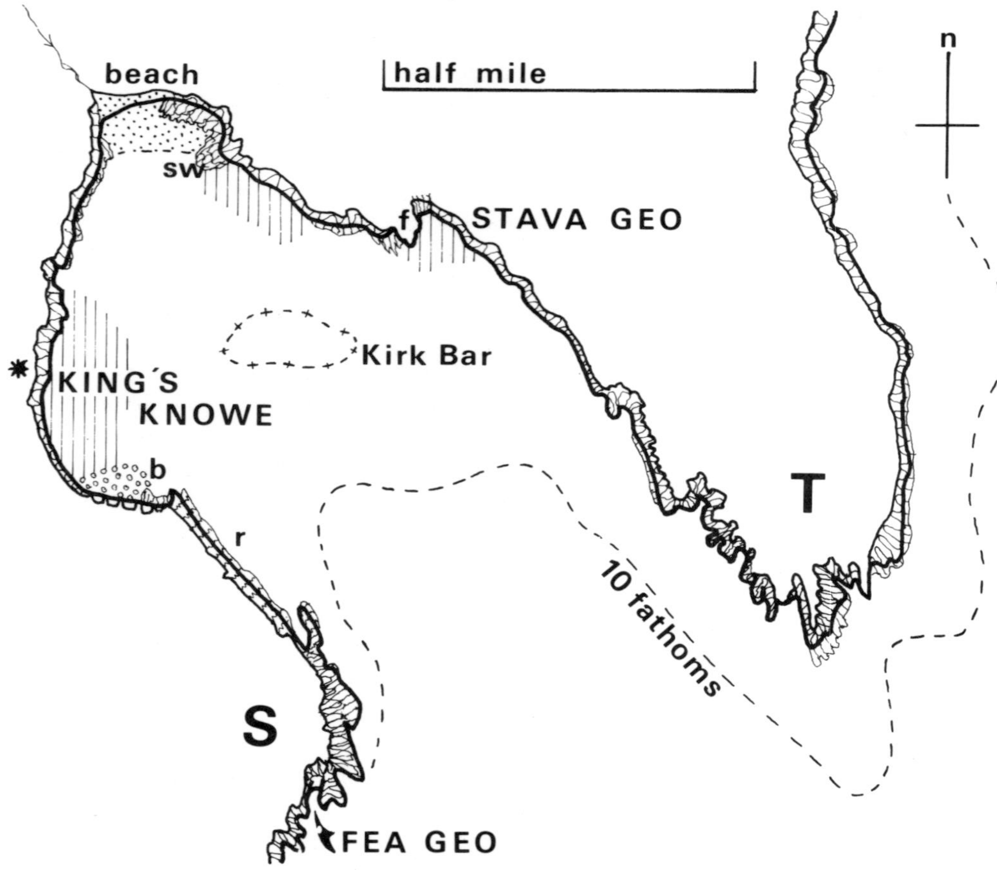

Gulberwick: the main search areas are ruled:
S. Setter Ness T. Trebister Ness b. boulder spread r. rock ramp sw. Swaart Skerries
j. fortification on the Hevdas

Opposite the Trebister cliffline on the other side of the bay, on the stretch of coast running in from Setter Ness, the rocks dip seawards and a great ramp of bedrock slabs sweeps down below present sea level. There seems no prospect of there being any kind of beach or cliff there in Viking times to satisfy the Saga. Furthermore, over much of that stretch the chance of any artefacts surviving on the storm-scoured slabs making up the seabed is in any case negligible. There thus seemed no need to tie up diver search resources there.

Other parts of the Gulberwick coastline were abandoned with more regret. These were the areas where the wrecks might well have occurred, but where the character of the seabed made effective search impracticable. There were three main places of this kind. These were the boulder filled bay below the steading of Setter, the sandbeach at the head of Gulberwick, and Fea Geo.

The bay below Setter lies at the inland end of the ramp section just discussed. There is evidence of very recent coastal erosion there (for example, the seaward dyke of a sheep pund is falling over an eroding sea scarp). This, together with the observations of people living around the bay, left no doubt that the massive spread of boulders that floors the shallows there is subject to continual reworking in the winter storms. It would be a good place to run ashore, and the stony beach and easily scaled scarp though certainly modified seem quite likely to have had similar predecessors there in Viking times. It would thus seem to fit the Saga satisfactorily, but, unfortunately, literally hundreds rather than tens of tons of boulders would have to be shifted to search there.

The sheer mass of the mobile material in the sand beach at the head of the bay presents a similar problem. The way that the Kirk Bar often causes seas to break has already been mentioned. Both Captain Inkster and Mr. Sales, a former coxwain of the Lerwick lifeboat who had often fished in Gulberwick, reckoned that *Hjolp* and *Fifa* could well have been overwhelmed on the bar, and then have been swept on to the beach. Furthermore, if control is retained, but one is forced to run one's craft ashore, it is by far the most attractive place in Gulberwick for which to head. Mr. Andrew Ridland whose croft overlooks Gulberwick, was once embayed by night in the Voe of Sound, in conditions very similar to those indicated by the Saga. He was able to make out the gleam of the beach despite the darkness, and managed to run the labouring boat ashore there. It was stove in, but those aboard and much of their gear came safely through the surf. Afloat in Gulberwick itself, Ian

Morrison found that even in the dark of night the lighter tone of the sand and the lower profile of the valley that runs back from it can often be distinguished from the gloom of the cliffs elsewhere.

The sand itself is however continually on the move. Within the six months preceding the Expedition, the beach proper was scoured away by a major gale, and then re-established itself. The shape of its offshore sand-bar changes even more often. What is more, while it seems very likely geologically that there was a similar bayhead beach in Viking times, this almost certainly lay further seawards. The geomorphological evidence of this received interesting corroboration from a local tradition passed on by Andrew Ridland's wife, Peggy. This was that there had been a patch of pasture immediately seawards of the east end of the present beach. Cows had once been picketed to graze where now there are only the scoured rocks of the Swaart Skerries. Elsewhere, it is by no means unknown for artefacts to be recovered from moving masses of sand. Indeed, often material from wrecks may appear, be reburied and reappear persistently as the sand recycles through repeated phases of erosion and redeposition. Remarkable finds have been made in such places by people who chanced to be in the right place at the right time, but to seek things systematically in such an area during the short span of an expedition requires more powerful metal detectors and excavation facilities than were available.

Ships in difficulty heading for the bayhead beach might very easily have failed to reach it, particularly if they had been swamped while crossing the Kirk Bar. In case they fetched up short of the beach (and also because this itself was probably further seawards then), the stretches of coastline and seabed running out from its present position were investigated on both sides of the bay. More attention was paid to the eastern side where conditions seemed to offer a greater chance of making finds. Jim Gill worked with what he called "the beady-eyed brigade", a group of experienced searchers headed by Richard Price and David Shaw, perhaps the most acute underwater observers on the whole Expedition. Pieces of wreckage were found but these all proved modern. The shallow well-scoured bedrock ledges did not offer good conditions for the preservation of artefacts.

Ian Morrision really thought that the Expedition's problems were over, when he heard of the placename "Fea Geo", out on Setter Ness. There are several cases in Shetland where coastal features have taken their names from shipwrecks, and in at least a couple of instances such names go back several centuries. Fifa Geo is a bit awkward to say, and a simplification down the years to Fea Geo would not be without precedent. Had Earl Harald's crew sensed that gap in the looming cliffs of the Ness, and thrust in there? Or, in an analogue of the Trebister Ness and Stava Geo situation, had they been trapped there while clawing northwards along the surf line?

A vessel swept into that cliff-girt slot in Setter Ness would certainly soon be smashed to pieces if there was any sea running. However, despite the forbidding aspect of the place, the crew would have a good chance of survival in the conditions indicated by the Saga. During full winter gales, enormous seas can toss whole tree trunks right out of the back of the Geo, fifty feet or more above sea level. On such days it would be lucky if even one or two men survived from a crew cast away there. It was however in the aftermath of a storm, rather than in the storm itself that the Saga indicates *Hjolp* and *Fifa* were lost. When conditions are not too extreme, the boulders that choke the inner end of the Geo offer a refuge at water level. Many of these broken rocks have fallen from above, so again they are compatible with either the landslip or the rocky-beach reading of *udr.* Once on the rocks, it is not difficult for determined men to climb up the back of the Geo. Indeed one day when the boat coming to pick them up was a bit late, Jim Gill, Denis Gauci and Ian Morrison among others decided that they were so "determined" to reach the dinner being cooked by Pam Butler at the Gulberwick Hall that they scaled the Geo in their diving gear and made their own way home.

Sadly, however, the sheer magnitude of the pile of tumbled boulders in the Geo, below as well as above the sea's surface, ruled out an effective search. It seems very possible that this mass may have been augmented by substantial cliff falls within the last millennium, and large quantities of rocks, many weighing several tons apiece, would have to be shifted if any conclusions were to be reached. Even a metal detector would not be much help, because modern metal wreckage was found jammed far into crannies between boulders well underwater.

The possibility that any material washed out of the seaward end of the Geo might have settled into deeper water, where it might be less subject to wave attack, was investigated. This sounds like a very academic way of spending a morning, but the diving around Fea Geo proved some of the most exhilarating of the Expedition, and this trip into the clear depth off the Ness was no exception. For reasons discussed in Chapter 7, the visibility underwater there was better than within Gulberwick, and indeed outstanding by most North Sea standards, and it is worth taking a break from the detective work to look through a diver's eyes at what was to be seen down there.

The divers submerged in the throat of the Geo itself. A lazy sunlit swell was rolling in and fulmars whipped by, turning their heads to watch us, their bellies brilliant white against the black crags overhead. We slid downwards, weaving our way gently between great fronds of glossy sundappled kelp. At first these were golden orange, seeming almost fluorescent in their contrast with the turquoise of the water beyond. Then, as we finned deeper, the sea above progressively filtered out the red end of the spectrum. Orange darkened to brown and brown became a shade of green, until at length we were in an almost entirely monochromatic blue-green world. Still pellucid and full of light, this had lost nothing in attractiveness. Indeed it possessed an other-worldly quality that tended to seduce one from "disciplined scientific observation".

So often the diver works in an arm's length world, pleased to be able to make out anything at all in the gloom encompassing him. Here instead we soared through long vistas, like birds in slow motion. The kelp-covered tumble of great blocks gave way to stretches of well rounded cobbles. Through these rose massive citadels of pale bedrock, with a sinuous solidity of line that would not have been out of place in a Gaudi cathedral. There was no sound except for the regular rush of compressed air into our mouths as we breathed, and the burble of our bubbles leaving on their long journey to the surface.

Men have always dreamed of flying, but in the sky rules, regulations and a complex technology tend to come between the pilot and the full joy of freedom in three dimensions. Divers groping in really low visibility often feel twinges of claustrophobia, and are more conscious of the weight of thick water pressing down upon them than of any freedom. Deep in the mouth of Fea Geo however one could hang in mid-water as in mid-air, and see to left and to right the massive buttresses supporting the opposing cliff faces. They loomed distant but clear through a transparent green shot with roving beams of silvery light. Hovering thirty feet above the seabed, with the weird landscape in sharp focus below, one could either breathe out and slide serenely down between the citadels and cathedrals, or breathe in and soar sunwards. In conditions like that, it was not unknown for flights of divers to pass doing synchronous slow rolls, or to follow each other through loops fit to grace Farnborough . . .

In terms of the more mundane business of selecting areas for

Peter Milne surveying on the sea bed

Above: *Helen Milne starts up the Strathclyde inflatable boat*

Left: *Dive boat over search area*

systematic searches, these reconnaissance dives off Fea Geo were less rewarding. They showed that there was little hope of finding anything that might have been washed out of the Geo itself and fallen into the deeper water beyond. The divers soon realised that the depths of water existing off the headland were simply not sufficient to place the seabed there beyond the reach of the kind of wave action Shetland experiences. Even in 90 feet of water it was clear that at any rate the bigger storms affected the bottom. Off Setter Ness this was gravel rather than sand, but it had still been worked into a great array of parallel ridges. Off Trebister Ness, Nic Ashmore found potholes in the bedrock that were apparently being actively scoured, and this too hinted at the power of the Shetland seas even at depth. In practical terms, then, outside as inside the Geo, the Expedition had regretfully to recognise that it was beyond their scope to make a meaningful search. Whether Fea is indeed an elision of *Fifa* must therefore remain an enigma, and we must continue to wonder whether the ugly boy earl scrambled up the cliffs there.

Only one major region of Gulberwick remains, but this was one possessing most of the qualities being sought. Along with Stava Geo, it was therefore selected for special attention by the Expedition. It lay off the King's Knowe, on the Setter side of the bay.

This area, first of all, seemed thoroughly compatible with the Saga. It offered feasible landing places on rock ledges. There were sporadic accumulations of shingle and boulders, and scalable cliffs. Furthermore, underwater the bedrock topography was complex, with many crevices, and these were often choked by the shingle or buried beneath the boulders. Conditions for artefact survival thus seemed relatively propitious, while the area remained susceptible to search with the type of equipment and personnel available.

As we have seen the whole problem of oral traditions was a vexed one because the Shetland interest in the Saga seems to have produced a crop of modern, ultimately book-based, speculations. However, Mr. Tom Henderson of the Museum could recall hearing old people associate the King's Knowe specifically with the site of the wrecking of "Earl Ronald", and there seemed some slim possibility that this might indeed reflect a genuine tradition among the older and now departed families of the Gulberwick area.

The name of the mound is however a problematic one. Unusually for Shetland, it is in English and since Rognvald certainly never appears to have been referred to as a king, it seems likely to Lucy Collings and Bob Farrell that the name has been derived from a corruption of a Norse topographic term *kinn*, and does not of itself imply a connection with the Earl.

The Knowe itself is also something of a puzzle. The Expedition made a survey of its external characteristics. Old amateur excavation trenches in its summit were cleaned, and the remains of stone structures there were recorded. The mound is capped by a platform of peaty turf, now partially destroyed, but its body is of sand and gravel. This may well be a natural deposit, although rabbit burrows in the broken top go down into relatively soft material, and the

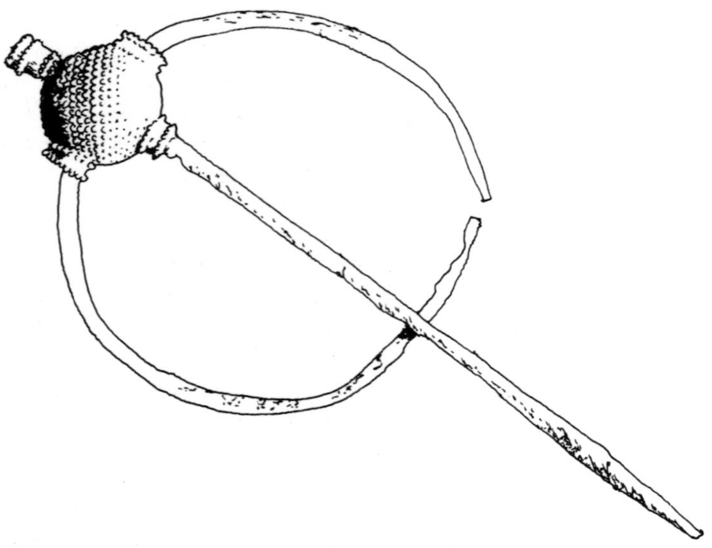

The Gulberwick Broocn

possibility of, say, a burial at the base level of the mound can not be eliminated without full excavation. Denis Mott went over the area with an archaeological prospecting instrument called a flux-gate magnetometer. This measured anomalies in the earth's magnetic field, but he considered that those that he found were too small for any positive conclusion to be reached.

The stone structures in the mound's top are so disturbed that it is not now clear what they represent. One long slab, set on edge, might possibly have been the side of a destroyed grave. A striking silver brooch, typical of Viking grave goods, is one of the treasures of the Museum in Lerwick. It is known as "the Gulberwick Brooch", and it is just conceivable that it came from here. It is said to have come to light long ago, when a boy was found preparing to melt it down to make a fishing sinker . . . he was apparently under the impression that the discoloured silver was lead. There are several alternative local traditions now as to where it was found, and the structure in the mound may not indeed have been a grave. There were occasional pieces of clinker, but this was not abundant enough to suggest a forge site and the Knowe is certainly not a "burnt mound", a common but perplexing type of artificial hillock of fired stones found in the Northern Isles. However, the possibility of some kind of beacon or leading-light arises in view of the remarkably precise positioning of the centreline of the mound (and indeed the alignment of the long slab) on the transect of Trebister Ness with the Bard o' Bressay.

This was all very intriguing, but the only way to put theories to the test was to get our ears wet. The underwater procedures used in the two main search areas, Stava Geo and King's Knowe, varied in detail because of differences in submarine topography, but the aim was the same in each case. This was simply to ensure that as far as possible nothing was missed. This was however more easily said than done. As has already been pointed out, there seemed no hope of finding large pieces of ship structure, nor was it likely that anything as massive and durable as the cannon of later centuries would have been aboard *Hjolp* and *Fifa*. It was therefore a matter of seeking small objects that had become buried or jammed down cracks in the bedrock, where they were likely to be camouflaged by algal growths, or entirely embedded in concretions that might well pass for natural pebbles or bedrock excrescences.

It might be thought that underwater metal detectors would provide the answer. Equipment kindly lent by Bradford and Oxford Universities was tried out, but in this case it did not solve the problem. It was better adapted to shallow sand spreads than the type of deep and narrow rock crevices encountered. Besides, the Shetlanders had taken countermeasures. From the vast number of beer cans discovered ashore there, the divers began to suspect that whatever the purpose in Viking times, the King of the Knowe in recent years has gone by the name of McEwan, and the concern there has been with Export rather than import of Earls. Car chassis and even cast-iron Victorian fireplaces added to the confusion for metal detectors.

The search thus fell essentially on the divers, and what they could achieve by direct observation. The aim being a really intensive "saturation search" of the chosen areas, the first necessity was to evolve some system that would ensure that we could keep track of exactly which pieces of seabed had been examined and which had not. If divers simply swarmed over the area, some work was likely to be reduplicated, and many of the less obvious nooks and crannies were sure to be missed.

A system of search corridors was therefore laid out on the seabed. In Stava Geo, the bedrock reefs split the underwater terrain into clearcut units, and divers led by Nic Ashmore worked down the intervening canyons, which were subdivided where necessary by ropes and tapes fixed in position on the bottom. The layout of the area was recorded underwater by Dr. Peter Milne of Strathclyde University, using his own special submarine survey method.

In the case of the King's Knowe site, the rock ridges were lower and more complex, and in general less suitable for use as a framework for the search. Under the direction of Alan Bax, pairs of ropes, set 5 metres apart and calibrated at 5 metre intervals along their length, were laid out at right angles to the shore. These ran for about a hundred metres seaward, since this was the distance that the original snorkel reconnaissance suggested as a reasonable search limit. The positions of the ends of the lines were surveyed in, by Pam Butler and Angela Bax using sextants. The Army divers experimented with an underwater bolt-firing gun to give secure anchor points in the bedrock.

The area to be tackled was a large one, some 300 metres long, so corridors were laid out simultaneously from seven control points along the shore. Fourteen divers could thus be working in pairs in the lanes at any given time without risk of confusion. As each corridor was finished, the westward line was leap-frogged over the eastward one. The fresh corridor, sharing the common line with the previous one, could thus be guaranteed to leave no intervening gap in the search. The leapfrogging was continued until the gaps between the control points were eventually filled in.

Because of the intensiveness and difficulty of the search, the divers often only got a few metres down their lanes on any one dive. Short cross lines were therefore moved along each corridor so that the next shift would know precisely where they were to take over. Each pair split their 5 metre wide lane between them, and the individual diver thus moved along exploring every possible hiding place on a 2½ metre wide front. Each carried an underwater writing pad of plastic paper on a board and kept a continuous log of his observations as he went. Sketches as well as written notes were made on the seabed, and the position of all man-made material that was found was plotted. This was done with waterproof fibreglass tapemeasures, using the

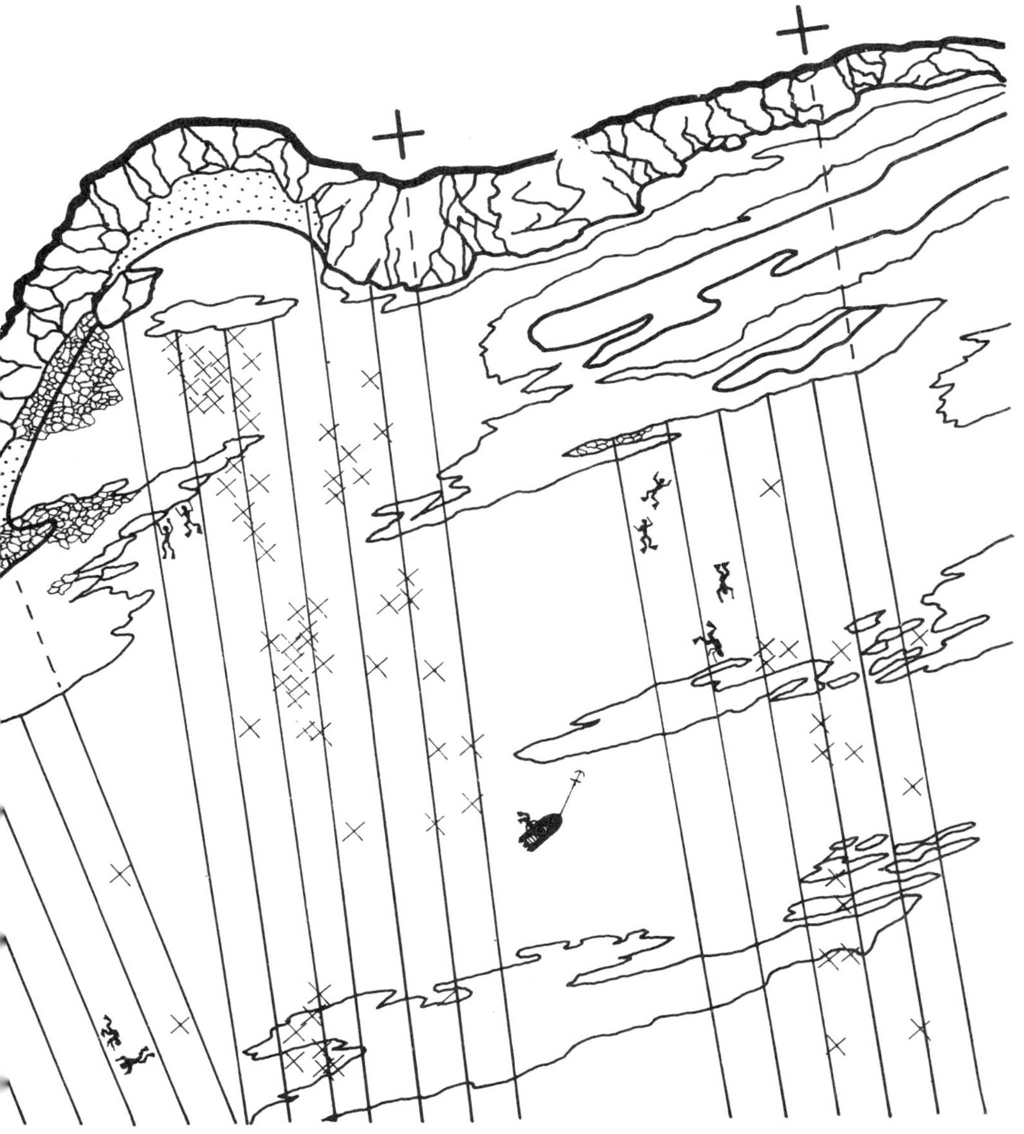

Search procedure: The divers are working in 5 metre wide lanes marked out with ropes on the sea bed, in relation to the cliff-top control points. The small crosses mark findspots of fragments of metal, wood, pottery, bone, etc.

marked lines for reference. Immediately on surfacing, the divers were given hot drinks and interrogated individually by the ladies of the non-diving support group. Their underwater notes were expanded then and there, for transcription into the full log that evening.

This kind of thing is just sheer hard work, but it is essential in a great deal of scientific and archaeological diving. Underwater, one tends to be preoccupied with the exigencies of the immediate situation, and after a long dive it is very easy to find that details are confused if no notes were taken as things actually occurred. The fact that the medium in which one is immersed can not be breathed is not (and should not be) far below the surface of one's mind. Even in the case of very experienced divers, indeed perhaps especially in their case, this subconscious awareness of being in a basically hostile environment influences the degree of concentration given to the task in hand, for the old sailor's principle of one hand for the ship and one for himself is a good one below the waves as well as above. This split in concentration between "work" and "survival" however tends to make divers live in a very "immediate" world while they are underwater. They notice things and grasp their direct importance, but fail to register longer-term or more subtle implications of their observations. This tendency seems to start far short of the depths associated with nitrogen narcosis, indeed many feel that it happens as soon as one submerges. Certainly, even in these shallow search operations the immediate de-briefings on landing helped greatly in capturing details, the potential significance of which had eluded immediate evaluation made on the seabed.

The daily compilation of the Expedition log served another vital purpose. On an operation of this scale, with up to thirty divers busy in their little patches of seabed, it was vital to maintain a clear picture of the overall pattern of the information emerging from the search, so that tactics could be modified and attempts made to optimise efforts from day to day. The divers' reports recorded the type of terrain they were encountering, as well as giving the co-ordinates of all man-made material found. The different categories of finds (worked wood, metal, pottery, etc.) were entered day by day on a map of the seabed. This was done for all such finds, including those that were manifestly modern, since this gave a picture of the way that objects were moving from the various cliff-side dumps. The distribution gave some idea of the way that the sea conditions in the bay interacted with local bottom topography, producing some zones in which objects accumulated while sweeping others clear.

Loose small finds were raised for examination by the professional archaeologists of the party. They were logged along with the co-ordinates from which they had come, and were preserved wet as a temporary measure. Arrangements had been made in advance of the Expedition for immediate museum-standard conservation of any finds that seemed to warrant it. Even now, despite the efforts of the Council for Nautical Archaeology, too many amateur groups make great efforts of organisation to run expeditions in quest of archaeological material but omit the complementary step of making proper provision for conserving what they find. This is just as vital, because objects immersed in sea or lake waters for long periods undergo physical and chemical changes, and to let them simply dry out can be disastrous. It is not just that wooden objects distort and break up, seemingly well preserved things of iron disintegrate. Even massive bronze cannons can moulder away with "bronze disease" and become worthless lumps of junk if removed thoughtlessly from the sea.

Larger finds, or those cemented by concretion to the rocks, were examined and photographed where they lay on the bed of Gulberwick. The careful survey of findspots meant that they could be located again there for further investigation if this seemed necessary. This meant that the possibility of damage or of incurring major conservation problems that might have arisen by raising them hastily could be avoided.

So much then, for the principles of the search. In practice, what was it like to be involved in an enterprise of this kind? The serried ranks of sleeping bags on the Hall floor would lurch into life around seven-thirty and the day would begin. A trailer load of cylinders would be towed off to the beach. These had been recharged with compressed air the night before, by Dennis Gauci's "back shift". A compressor was often kept working through the day on site too, to keep the successive waves of divers supplied. Most did at least two long dives during the day. Those who were scheduled for the first wave would aim to be at the beach, kitted up and launching the inflatable boats not long after the trailer arrived. Outboards would putter into life and they would head out over the swell to the search area,the headlands of Gulberwick grey and green in the morning light.

Through the day, the scene on the beach would be a busy one. The two little sons of Joyce in the cottage there watched with great interest, but like good Shetlanders showed little sign of being impressed by the antics of the Sooth-Moothers. They did however seem to approve when two-year-old Robert Milne hove into view clad as a tiny frogman. His miniature wet suit had been tailored from a spare length of neoprene by Helen and Peter, his amphibious parents.

Bob Farrell generally acted as beach-master, co-ordinating the administrative details that had to be taken into account if fresh divers, air supplies and fuel were to be ready for dispatch when the boats came back. Inevitably, with up to thirty divers on the go at any one time and several types of specialised gear in use there were crises from time to time.

Denis Mott had the art of materialising then, brandishing some improbable but invaluable implement from his seemingly inexhaustible tool-box. From his way of bounding into sight in his Landrover and then swinging down and taking charge of a problem with an authoritative cry of "Right . . . ", one lady from an American university formed the impression that he was part of the British Army team. This was realised when she commented on viewing him in action that you could certainly see why he had made Colonel so young . . . His cap had added to the confusion, but this much prized relic had more to do with steam engines than Sandhurst. On reflection, we decided that the mistake was not only to the credit of Denis as a man of action, but also to that of the genuine article for the unobtrusive tact with which he shared the responsibility for a principally civilian Expedition!

Crises even had their philological aspects. The usage of the word Viking was significantly extended by the Expedition. There comes a moment in dealing with recalcitrant machinery when neither technological finess nor brute strength will prevail, and words come forth. That moment came to Martin Dean while he strained to loosen a jammed fire-hose coupling. Glancing up to utter, his muscles creaking, he realised he was surrounded by the ladies of the Expedition, all solicitous, and what came out was "This is *Viking* tight . . . " The substitution rapidly became general.

There was much over which the divers might mumble. Sometimes the seabed problems of the search reminded Ian Morrison of a difficult day working off the Out Skerries on a previous expedition. The wreck there was in ten fathoms and those in the boat certainly could not see the divers at work below. Yet when he surfaced, they asked him what all the trouble had been about. When asked how they had known about it, the laconic reply was that they had read the words in his bubbles.

The first problem in Gulberwick was the thick growth of kelp that shrouded the reefs. It is often referred to in Scotland as "tangle", and this is very appropriate. Underwater, its broad dark fronds shut out the light and have the knack of plastering themselves across divers faceplates. It can stand man high, on stalks as thick as one's wrist. If the divers harvested it with their daggers, the calm conditions that were so helpful to the Expedition in other respects meant that unless laboriously dragged clear of the search area, the weed would lie for days in great swathes, choking the canyons between the reefs.

Then, having located cracks in the rocks one would find that many of the most promising ones for catching and sheltering small objects were jammed with seemingly inextricable pebbles, cemented firmly into place. Could these be protecting a lump of concretion? Something might be sensed lurking behind them at the back of the crevice. Much levering and perhaps a fingernail or two later, a way would be cleared and the anomalous looking nodule would be extracted, surveyed in, logged on the underwater notepad, and bagged for later examination on the surface. Then the next cranny would be sought, and groped as far as the arm would reach. The cold anaesthetised the barnacle tears on the hands, but one would find out about them later.

To protect the neoprene of their wet suits in this kind of work, some of the divers wore boilersuits over the top. The old Expedition hands of the permanent staff had not been so injudicious as to bring new gear in the first place, and after a couple of months of this type of diving, Richard, Dave and Ian looked every inch the submarine beach-combers that they had become. Fringed fetlocks of neoprene that had once been diving bootees were replaced by superannuated gymshoes, patches patched patches and tapes taped tape. All in all, they could hardly be said to have come up to those standards of submarine sartorial excellence set by the glossy diving magazines.

Between the rock ridges, the gullies were often choked by boulders. Sometimes instead there was sand or shingle. Since the Shetland storms were likely to shift these infills, the divers had to attempt to do this too, so that they could inspect the crevices in the bedrock beneath. They soon became adept at creating "windows" in thin sand layers by fanning currents of water with their hands. For shifting shingle, ordinary coal-shovels and buckets were used, and the homely scene on the seabed off the King's Knowe was completed by the arrival of the underwater vacuum cleaner. This had been improvised one afternoon at Fort Bovisand by Nic Ashmore. A portable firepump, overhead in an inflatable, fed water under pressure down a hose to the device. There the highspeed small-bore jet from the hose was squirted up the inside of a large bore plastic drainpipe . . . dragging a column of water with it, and giving enough suction at the bottom of the tube to clear sand.

Since not even Nic was considered wicked enough to be condemned to vacuum clean the entire bay, experiments were made with ways of choosing places to dig the holes. The problems with the metal detector surveys of this particular area have already been mentioned. An interesting alternative approach was tried out by Peter Milne and Dave Grant in one of the larger sand patches below the Knowe. They used hand probes to measure the depth of sand, and plotted the positions of the probed points using Peter's underwater plane table. It was then an easy matter to draw a contour map showing the configuration of the bedrock buried beneath the sand. This map then let the burrowers know precisely what to expect.

Things more heroic in scale than sand grains were shifted underwater. The Bradford crew in particular specialised in hoisting great boulders skywards. They did this by hitching them to an inverted dustbin, then puffing compressed air into this until the whole lot took off. It will be noted that the technology of Inner Space had a distinctly domestic air once again. It was however highly effective, for most rocks, though they manifestly do not float, have a density only two to three times that of water, and hence effectively weigh very much less when immersed. When one remembers also that even a fair sized biscuit tin can displace a cubic foot of water and give the better part of half-a-hundredweight of lift, the scope of Bradford dustbin-power may be appreciated. And it was not left only to the lads. A mermaid by the name of Val performed extraordinary feats on the seabed, and elsewhere.

What all these efforts showed was that modern material could be found right down to the bottom of the gully infills, wherever holes were dug. This confirmed that the pattern observed by the Gulberwick people around the shore of the bay in fact prevailed throughout the search area. They had often seen the really big winter storms clear the gullies between the reefs right down to bedrock. In many cases the detailed shape of the canyon walls underwater bore this out, for these had been smoothly undercut by the abrasion of moving shingle. This was even more noticeable in the Stava Geo search area than at the King's Knowe.

From things such as these it became progressively more evident that any artefact recovered from the gullies was likely to be so rolled and abraded as to be virtually, or indeed wholly, unrecognisable. Looking at the myriads of fragments of artificial material that the search had yielded, one could not help but wonder whether some of them had not indeed come from *Hjolp* or *Fifa.* Such speculations are however unprofitable. The real result of the King's Knowe and Stava Geo searches was to demonstrate that short of the extraordinary luck of finding something that not only had lodged in the shelter of a crevice, but had done so almost immediately after shipwreck, archaeologically useful finds were not going to be made there, any more than in the more obviously unpropitious areas of the bay.

This conclusion was a sad one indeed, and one that was not fully accepted until the final days of boulder lifting disclosed the full extent to which storms turned over even heavy material, well up the bay. The thoroughness of the divers was not wasted however. It established this conclusion sufficiently firmly to make it clear that the conditions for artefact survival were unlikely to be any better in the Voe of Sound and the East Voe of Quarff. The range of underwater terrain represented there is too similar. As pointed out earlier the decision to concentrate on Gulberwick was made on operational grounds, and did not imply that the possibility of the wrecks taking place in the other bays could be disregarded. It would seem however from the Gulberwick results that it is not realistic to expect that further expeditions to any of the three bays could readily add much to the basic conclusion reached at the end of the last chapter. The situation on the seabed that makes positive archaeological proof of the wrecks highly unlikely at the same time forbids one to draw any definite negative conclusions regarding the wreck sites from the search attempts. Those who spent most time on the seabed at Stava Geo and the King's Knowe are the ones most aware of how easily the two Viking ships could have been wrecked even there and left no detectable trace.

It seems then that the general conclusion that local sea conditions and coastal characteristics appear thoroughly compatible with the Saga account is about as far as we can go with real confidence at the moment. The hours spent working beneath the waters of Gulberwick suggest that it may never be possible to get much further.

With obscurity still enveloping the precise site of the wrecking of the Earls, it is perhaps fitting that we leave the area as they came, in the dark. To be precise, with a night dive. The days of cold, boring, meticulous work by the successive teams of volunteers should not be under-estimated. Happily, however, it is not the humdrum discomforts of the routine working dives that stick in the memory of the participants, so much as moments like that off Fea Geo. Then one is suddenly reminded that by going into the sea one has entered an alternative world that can on occasion be as strange and as rich in visual experience as any likely to be encountered by the gentlemen of NASA. For some, it was a night dive on the Kirk Bar out in the centre of Gulberwick that provided the most memorable experience of the trip to Shetland.

It was late in the Expedition, and real darkness had returned. It was a beautifully clear night with stars everywhere, and leaning on the wall outside Gulberwick Hall we could hear the quiet sea lapping the beach below. The slow grind of the search had implanted a restlessness, and despite their long hours in the water in Stava Geo, the Tyneside team in particular were seeking more rather than less diving. What they wanted was some variety. Suddenly we were scrounging about, borrowing underwater lamps from the bedward brigade.

Eider duck shuffled grumpily off the beach as the divers materialised in the gloom bearing the boats down from their night-time resting place at the back of the sands. The sea was almost calm, and the outboards burbled peacefully at half throttle as we slid seawards, trying not to wake the cottagers. Though there was no moon then, the loom of the cliffs could be sensed and soon the boats were anchored well out in the bay in about five fathoms, near the Bar.

We slipped over the side, swimming in pairs as usual, each responsible for the other's safety. Hanging from the surface by the boat, we turned our diver's torches on and sent long fingers of light groping down into the clear black water. Ten feet beneath us fish slid past, scales gleaming in the beam. We headed downwards. Quite suddenly a yellow-grey saucer came into view, then grew into a soup plate. This was the narrow beam, hitting the sandy bottom. We arrived and lay still, torches held horizontal. They picked out the ripple-marks, and threw the delicately fanning fronds of seaworms into sharp silvery relief against the black beyond. A quick sweep with the beam caught the anchor rope, still clustered with bubbles like little spheres of mirror. With this as a departure point, a compass course was laid to take us the last lap towards the Bar itself.

We cruised slowly over the silvery sand, watching the shadows in the ripple-marks change as we moved. Then the torches, scanning ahead, picked up a forest. This was the edge of the kelp jungle that grew over the rocky reefs of the Kirk Bar proper, and that night it was an enchanted forest indeed.

For the diver daylight under any depth of water is not only virtually monochromatic but diffuse. The diffusion is always present, and can even become so marked that our land-conditioned perceptual system can run into trouble. Sometimes in deep clear water, even under the strong light of the Mediterranean, the diffusion can be so complete that one feels at the centre of an evenly lit blue-green ball. All normal visual reference may be lost then, and like a helicopter pilot beset by a "white-out" in the Arctic (when snowy ground and sky become indistinguishable) the diver may have to "fly on instruments" and keep an eye on where his bubbles are going, to know "up". This extreme example has been given to emphasise how marked the diffusion of light is underwater. When he is in touch with the seabed or surface, no problems of orientation draw the diver's attention specifically to the quality of the lighting. Nevertheless he soon becomes conditioned to regard shadowless, non-directional illumination as one of the most familiar characteristics of his environment down there. Almost without realising why, he may be intrigued, or indeed almost shocked, into a sense of extra awareness if plunged into different conditions.

That is what happened that night. For weeks we had been working in the flat-lit kelp tangle of day time, going there with the same regular routine and general lack of exhilaration that we knew so well as office-bound commuters during the rest of our year. Now, abruptly the all-too-familiar kelp office had undergone a strange sea change. Light from our torches roved through the three-dimensional blackness, opening up glades in the jungle or suddenly revealing the gleam of a browsing fish at the end of a tunnel through the tall stalks. A crab, huge in the spotlight, went lurching off sideways down an alleyway. As a pair of divers moved in pursuit, their torches first sent shadows flickering across the wide fronds of the nearer weed, then faded into a silvery glow half seen through a silhouetted tracery of stalks. To keep in touch, we slid up through the canopy of the forest, and hung in the dark water above. Below, they themselves were invisible in the blackness, but the cones of their lights split and flickered as they moved down an overgrown canyon.

We swooped down again, and for a little sped low and fast over the kelp-clad ridges, like hedge-hopping pilots. We used our torches as headlamps, and snaked over or around the great clumps of golden forest that came hurtling towards us out of the black beyond. We ran into a country of crags, cast into high relief by the unaccustomed harshness of the artificial light. Stopping finning, we drifted down our light beams into a rocky rift, fascinated by the brilliant yellows and reds the torches were conjuring from the algae on the stone walls. In the depth-filtered light of day, these would have been grey-green.

Our gauges said air was running low. We picked up the edge of the forest and followed it back to a crag that identified our entry point, then set off in a shallow climb on the reciprocal of our original compass course. The compasses were luminous, and we switched off our lights. As our eyes adjusted, we became aware that towards the surface the water was full of phosphorescent plankton. We took turns following each other, watching the patterns we were creating. The man himself was invisible, but the regular beat of his swimming disrupted the star-clouds streaming past. Rhythmically with each stroke vortices spurted from the edges of his flippers. These whipped the pinpoints of light together then released them in three dimensional spirals, decelerating as they dispersed. We cruised just under the surface, fascinated and spinning out our air as long as it would last.

The whole dive had been so delightful that we felt sorry for the stand-by divers and boat-handlers waiting at anchor above, on safety duty. They were probably bored to tears up there by now. We surfaced and found that this was anything but the case.

Soon after we had emerged, the whole dome of the sky over them had become suffused with the Aurora Borealis. It was still in progress, and instead of crowding aboard we inflated our life jackets, thumbed our masks back, and swung gently in the black swell watching too. Enormous veils of the lightest and palest silk drifted far above us, falling into evanescent pleats or dissolving and reforming for minutes on end. It was a happy group indeed who supped Pam's soup at the head of the beach before heading for their sleeping bags.

The search of Gulberwick certainly had its boring and frustrating side, and the cheery determination and sheer endurance of the volunteers who carried it through more than impressed the professionals in the team. In experiences like those at Fea Geo and the Kirk Bar, however, Shetland offers much that compensates for the less attractive side of the work involved in this kind of Expedition.

Let us now leave the northerly bays and head south with Earl Rognvald.

Chapter 6

The Earl Incognito and the Tide-Race – Detective Work at Jarlshof

After the shipwreck Earl Rognvald stayed in Shetland for quite a long period before returning south to his headquarters in Orkney. He seems to have spent part of his time moving around, getting the feeling of his northern dominions, and sometimes at least he travelled incognito. He may have done this in order to gauge for himself how far he might expect trouble in the area in the future. In other words, he may have gone in disguise to find out how far what was said behind his back departed from what was said to his face. Alternatively he may simply have wanted to avoid fuss and attention. We have no way of knowing now, but if his aim was the latter one, it certainly rebounded upon his head, if the Saga is to be believed, the day he went to Dynrastarvág.

This is what the Saga calls the place. Dynrost is the old name for the tide-race or Roost that flows past Sumburgh Head at the southern tip of Shetland, and from this the parish of Dunrossness has taken its name. It will be remembered that it was in the Dunrossness Hall that the Expedition was based for much of its stay.

On the morning that he came there, according to the Saga, fishing was in progress, and boats were leaving the beach and being rowed out seawards as soon as their crews were ready. One poor old man had a long wait. The word used for him is "bondi", but for convenience we shall refer to him as a "crofter", intending by this simply one who both farms and fishes, and sidestepping the more technical connotations of both terms since these do not affect what follows. At length a fellow enveloped in a white cloak with a cowl came up to him and asked him why he did not set off like the others.

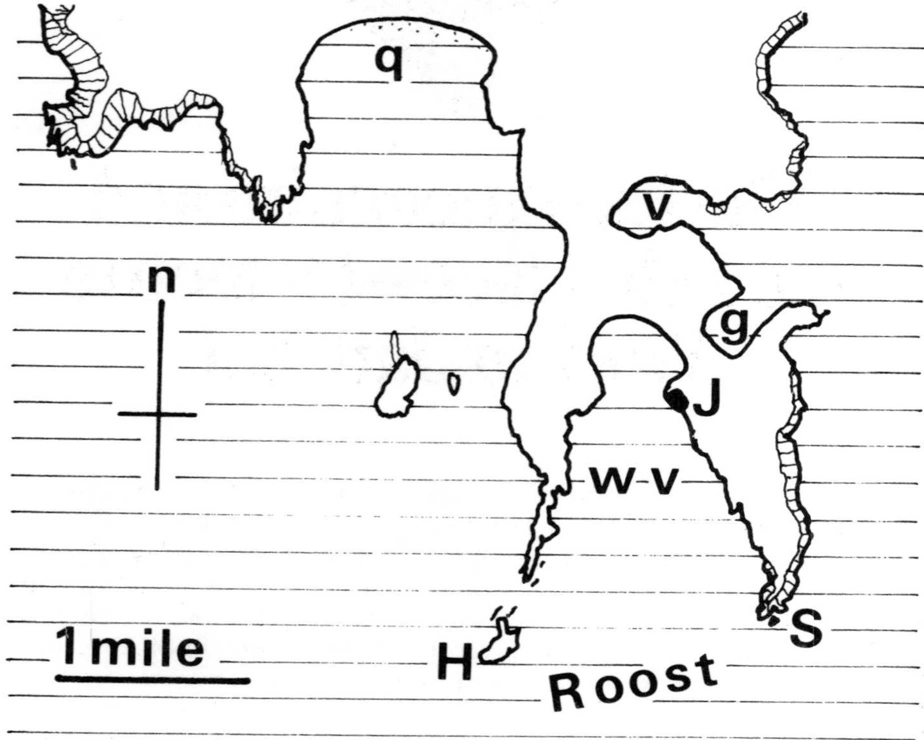

J. Jarlshof H. Hundholm S. Sumburgh Head q. Quendale Bay v. Pool of Virkie g. Grutness Voe wv. West Voe of Sumburgh

Leaving the surface

Clearing kelp jungle during the seabed search

Above: *The best preserved of the surviving brochs, on Mousa, with Sumburgh in the background*

Below: *Jarlshof, with the rock platform and the sea wall protecting the remains of the broch. The tall ruin is the Laird's House visited by Sir Walter Scott*

The crofter, unaware that this was Rognvald, explained that his mate had not arrived. "Crofter", says the man in the cowl, "will you let me row with you?"

"I will that", says the farmer, "though I must have my share of the boat's catch, for I've a lot of children at home".

They set off, and the Saga tells us that they rowed out before Dynraster Head and Hundholm into an area of strong currents. Dynraster Head is the modern Sumburgh Head, while Hundholm appears to be what is now known as Horse Island, guarding the other side of the entrance to the bay. The old name survives on 17th century Scottish and Dutch maps.

The headland and island are the most southerly points of the Shetland archipelago. The considerable north-south extent of the islands sets a barrier between the tidal circulations of the North Sea to the east and the Atlantic to the west, and rips and races develop here, as at the north end of the group. However, though strong, the currents flowing in the Roost of Scaw at Lamba Ness and in the area of the Muckle Flugga, both at the north end of Unst, are not of the same order as those to be encountered off Sumburgh. Even on a calm day, the race there may be heard from afar, and when a heavy sea is running wind and tide can combine to create a maelstrom that even powerful modern warships treat with respect.

Despite the dangers of these races, they have been favoured by fishermen from Viking times to the present day. The larger saithe frequent them (otherwise one must often seek these in deeper waters far off shore), while the Sumburgh Roost is one of the few places where it is still economic to go after halibut by long-line fishing.

The Dunrossness men have traditionally gone after the saithe in the type of slim yole described in Chapter 3. These were usually three-man craft, and the two rowed hard up tide while the third fished with a line towing a piece of skinned saithe or herring.

It seems that these Ness men used (and sometimes even yet, use) the very same method of fishing that Earl Rognvald took part in, in those same waters eight and a quarter centuries ago. The Saga reports that when they got out beyond the shelter of the headland and Hundholm, there was a strong current, with broad eddies. The aim was to hold the boat safely in the eddy and to fish in the tide-race. The man with the crowl sat in the bow and rowed against the tide, while the crofter did the actual fishing.

The local man, knowing his water, told his oarsman to take care not to let them be carried into the race, since that would be running great risks. Soon afterwards, however, they did drift into it. Whether

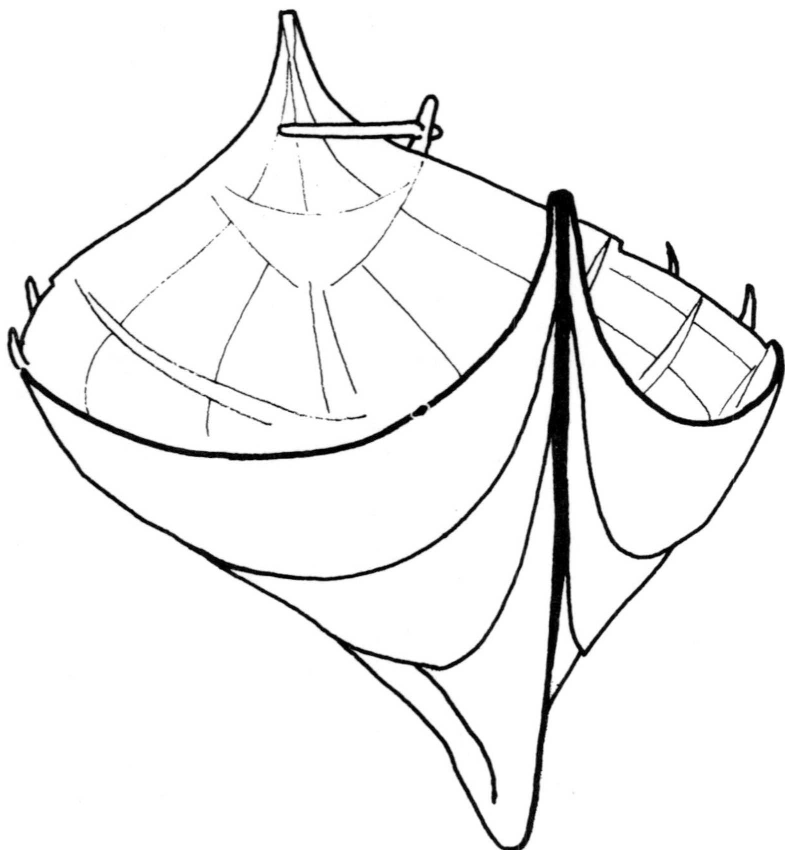

Small Viking Yole found with the Gokstad ship burial. The boat Rognvald took into the tide race was probably like this.

this was due to incompetence on the part of the Earl or whether, as the Saga writer would clearly prefer us to believe, he let it happen "for kicks" we shall never know now. What the Saga says is that the man with the cowl did not behave as he had been told, and cared nothing for the risk to the crofter.

The latter bemoaned his luck at having taken on such a crewman, envisaging his folk at home being reduced to beggary with no one left to fend for them. The man with the cowl told him to cheer up "for he who got us into the race shall pull us out again".

Some of the Expedition team working on the submarine geomorphology of Sumburgh one morning decided to take a judicious look at the Roost, to see what Rognvald and the farmer had been up against. Clearly the facts that the Viking fishermen had been working along its edges that day, and that Rognvald had been able to extricate himself single-handed under oars, meant that the race had been in one of its milder moods. We chose similar conditions, and lurked along the edge in the eddies, keeping clear of the race proper as the fishermen did, and as the Earl should have done. For all that it was a bright and almost windless day, the sight was an impressive one. First the colour of the water changed, then there were whirls and looping strings of foam. We noticed that the seals had stopped following our boat, though they were still watching us, lifting in the slow oily swell. Then along a quite definite burbling line we came to the shear plane between the still water inside the Voe and the fast flowing river-in-the-sea skirting outside headland and island. The bottom was more than twenty fathoms down, but the race had rapids and over-falls as if it was a brawling stream with rocks just below the surface. The familiar grey-green of the sea of the Voe had taken on a whitish tinge, with the masses of tiny bubbles sucked into the water by the turbulence. Puffs of spray whipped unexpectedly into the still air where disorderly waves met. We decided that Rognvald's brawn had been in better shape than his brain that morning.

Rognvald at last prevailed and they rowed ashore. They beached the boat, and the much-relieved crofter invited him to help himself to the fish. But the disguised Earl refused to take more than his one-third crewman's share and this he distributed to poor folk in the crowd who had come down to the beach to see the return of the boats. If all happened as the Saga says, this anonymous benevolence must surely have given him some slight glow of self-righteous pride . . . and pride comes before a fall.

There was a steep sea-bank behind the beach, and this was slippery after rain. As he went up it he lost his footing and to the amusement of women sitting along the bank, he slid precipitately down to the bottom again. We may guess that his landing was less than dignified, (and his cloak less white than when he had set out) for first one woman and then the rest of the crowd burst into laughter at him. He apparently felt rather piqued at this, after his generosity and his exploit in the race, for he came out with the following lines:—

The Sif of Silk mocks my garb;
Too much she laughs at me —
Few can tell an Earl, clad as a fisherman
But early in the morning
I rowed Húnn's oak valiantly over the waves.

The Sif, or goddess, of silk refers sarcastically to the woman, and Húnn's oak is perphrasis for the boat. This verse is believed to be the source of the Norse proverb that few recognise an earl in fishing clothes.

Having delivered himself of this, he went off, and it was only later that it was learned for sure who he had been. The Saga writer adds, rather sanctimoniously one feels, that after that, many men learned of many of his feats that were helpful before God and pleasant before men.

The crofter whose boat he had rowed, or almost certainly some others among those who fished that morning, may well have lived in the settlement we now call Jarlshof. This lies near the head of Dynrastarvág, or as it is now known, the West Voe of Sumburgh. The name "Jarlshof" has a fine Norse ring, but it is not original. It is the product of nineteenth century romanticism. Walter Scott visited Shetland towards the end of the Napoleonic Wars, and was struck by the gaunt and picturesque ruin of the 16th and 17th century house of the Lairds of Sumburgh, overlooking the Voe. He named it Jarlshof, and used it as the setting for part of his historical novel *The Pirate*. What he did not realise was just how accurate he was being in giving the site a Norse-sounding name. Under the blown sand that he had walked through at the ruin lay the remains of a settlement that had been occupied by several generations of Vikings, from the ninth century on through the time of Earl Rognvald.

This was not all. A series of archaeological investigations in the present century have revealed that, as the report by J.R.C. Hamilton puts it, "In Jarlshof Shetland possesses one of the most remarkable archaeological sites ever excavated in the British Isles . . . " On the sandy flats at the head of the Voe, successive layers of old habitations were buried and preserved by the gradual build-up of occupation debris and blown sand. The result was a comprehensive record of the past, more like the "tels" of the Middle East and Anatolia (where successive mudbrick settlements have built up into great mounds) than what the excavator can usually hope for in British conditions. Certainly, after a dozen seasons on excavations in Britain and abroad, the only sites offering a comparable length of record that Ian Morrison had worked on were located far off in the eastern Mediterranean.

The bottom layer of the Jarlshof mound tells of a time probably in the second millennium B.C. when the islanders were still essentially "Stone Age" in their lifestyle, though elsewhere in Britain bronze was already in use. Later, a hamlet of oval courtyard houses

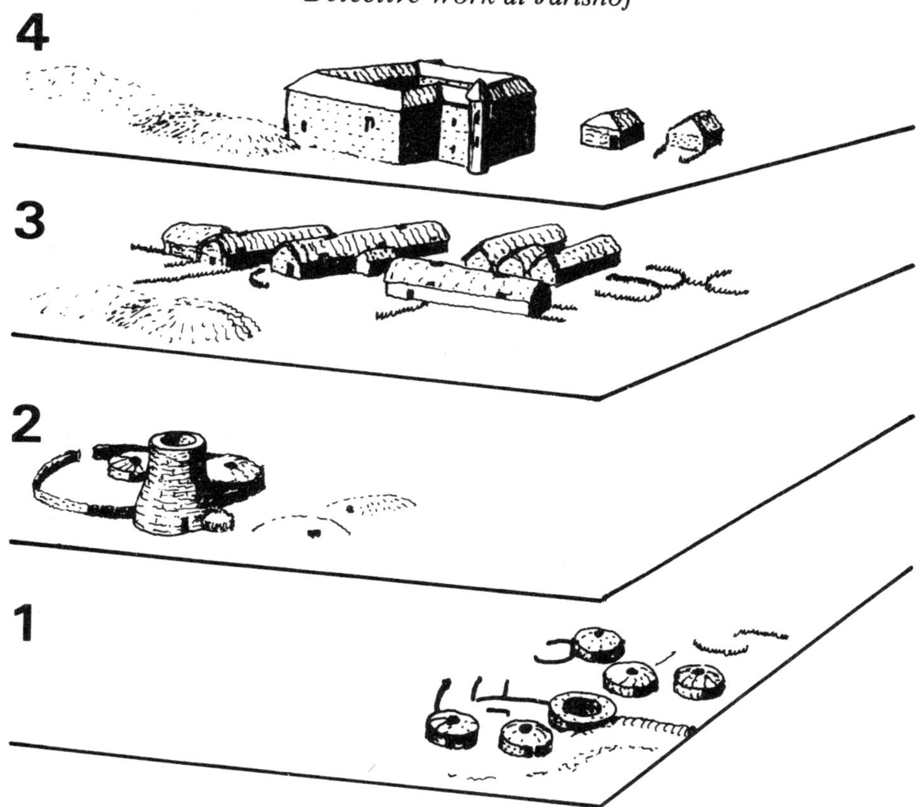

Jarlshof in 1: the Bronze Age. 2: the Iron Age. 3: the Viking era. 4: Mediaeval period.

developed, and local bronze working began. This village was in turn superseded by one of large circular houses supported by internal radial buttresses. By then, iron was being worked. During the Iron Age, a great "broch" became the keypoint of the settlement. Brochs are works of passive defence, heavy though not ungraceful round towers of carefully fitted dry-stone masonry with no windows and only one tiny door. Their profiles are not unlike a modern cooling tower. The one at Jarlshof may originally have been more than forty feet tall, like one that survives nearby, on the island of Mousa. They were still occupied while the Romans came and went to the south, and further houses with internal piers, this time with a distinctive wheel-like plan, were added around the Jarlshof broch in the centuries before the Vikings arrived. They came sometime around the start of the ninth century A.D., and their settlement of typical long rectangular cottages and byres went through successive renewals and expansions until it went into decline in the century after Rognvald's visit to the area. It was succeeded by a medieval farmstead. This in turn gave way to the Laird's house Sir Walter Scott dubbed "Jarlshof".

The story of the Viking occupation at Jarlshof runs through the better part of five centuries, and is fairly complex with buildings falling out of use, being regrouped or replaced, or sometimes refurbished so that they could be used for other purposes. The general pattern is clear however. The buildings were of the long low thatched rectangular type typical of the Viking world, found by archaeologists from Scandinavia west through the islands to Iceland, Greenland, and now indeed Newfoundland. The major ones at Jarlshof were quite substantial, with lengths running up to 70 feet, and widths around 20 feet. They were surrounded by smaller outhouses, and the whole complex included besides dwelling houses, barns, byres, stables and even what looks suspiciously like a little sauna bath-house. There are signs of a smithy, and hundreds of loom weights show that a lot of weaving went on, using tall vertical looms of the kind that were still to be seen in Norway and the Faroes until quite recently. Many of these weights, and the numerous fishing line sinkers found, were made of steatite, that is, soapstone. This was a favourite material of the Vikings for bowls and hanging lamps too, and an outcrop in Shetland was one of the major sources. There, at Cunningsburgh between Jarlshof and Lerwick, one can still see the cores on the rocks from which bowls were cut, and great piles of waste material.

Jarlshof around Earl Rognvald's time

It is difficult to be entirely sure when differing phases of rebuilding and repair were completed, but on the day that Rognvald went fishing the settlement may well have looked rather like the sketched reconstruction. As indicated in Chapter 2, its general appearance, the way the buildings were put together and indeed much of the farming and fishing gear around the place would not have seemed unfamiliar to Shetlanders (or Norwegians) who lived into our present century.

One thing that certainly was different, however, at the Jarlshof of Viking days, was the line of the coast. Some gales send heavy seas rolling up the Voe to pound the shoulder where the site stands. Ian Morrison saw something of this one snowy spring day in 1973 when he flew in to Sumburgh to join Owen Gander for some research work on sea level change. The cloud base was low and the Viscount kept under it on the last leg up from Kirkwall in Orkney, giving a superb view of the seascape below. Sheets of spume unwound from the tops of rollers and swept off downwind like veils of grey silk. Trawlers materialised out of the off-white blindness of snow squalls. They curvetted like stately horses, keeping dry decks by throwing great rhythmic clouds of spray outwards from their flaring bows as they nosed to windward. Slate-grey seas erupted in white explosions against the black crags of Fair Isle. Yet through all this, fishing gannets sped below. Sumburgh Head came into sight, then vanished in a squall. The pilot turned out to sea, orbiting well clear of the invisible bulk of Fitful Head and Ward Hill until the snow thinned. Then his approach skimmed in from the west, low across Rognvald's Hundholm. On the Atlantic side, the seas were breaking so heavily that there was a solid belt of surf for almost a quarter of a mile off shore. Things were better inside the protection of the headlands, but as the Viscount slid even lower across the Voe it was clear that no mean sea was running there too. The final turn northwards, into a nicely judged cross-wind landing, pivoted round Jarlshof itself. Great slow breakers were pounding the sea wall at the site with sullen concussions, and as it slid past the dipping wing-tip, the old grey shell of the Laird's House was abruptly engulfed in a whiff of spray.

The sea wall was built specially to preserve the site from further erosion. The buried settlements there first came to the attention of archaeologists when a series of storms at the end of the nineteenth century started tumbling sections of massive stone walls out of the sea-bank onto the beach. One aim of the Expedition was to see whether there was any prospect of finding out how big the site had been originally. Archaeologists were also interested to know whether divers might be able to recover anything from the eroded portion.

The results of the erosion are spectacular. The broch is the most substantial structure at Jarlshof, and it has been cut almost exactly in half. The Iron Age structures that flank it have also been laid open on the seaward side. None of the surviving Viking buildings, to landward of the broch, have been damaged, but it seems quite likely that others have been totally lost. For example, the finding of so many fishing sinkers and the fishing scene in *Orkneyinga Saga* both imply that many boats were in use. The Vikings built boat-shelters of a kind very common in Shetland up to recent times and now known as noosts (naustr in Old Norse), yet those belonging to the settlement have not been found.

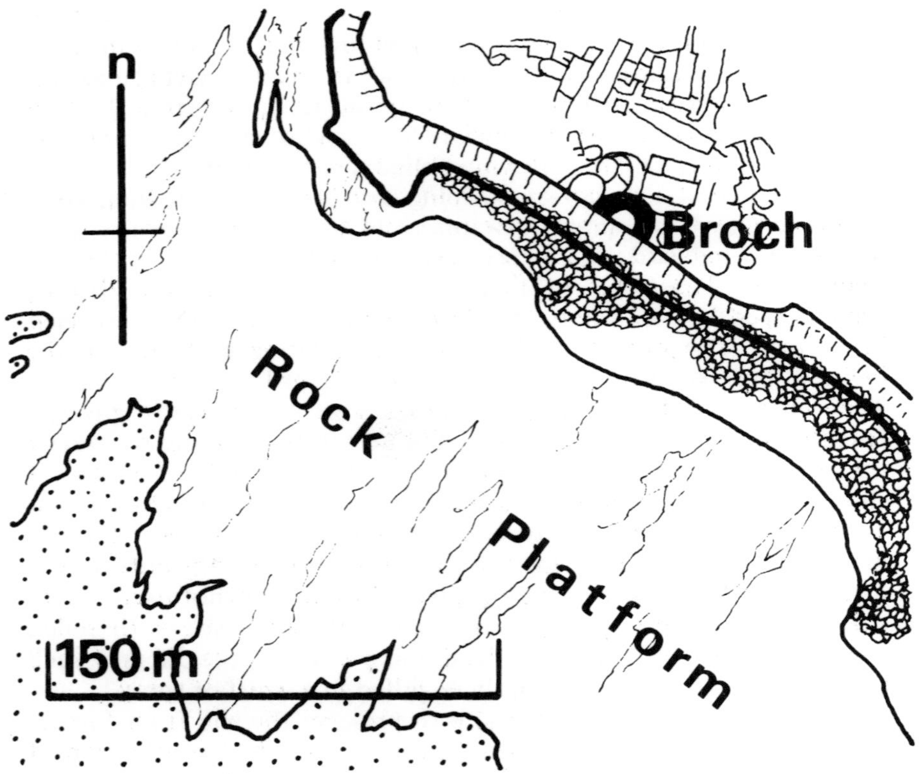

The present eroded state of Jarlshof, and the underwater rock platform.

Even a superficial examination of the site suggested that there was no hope of tracing the remains of buildings underwater. In Greece or

Italy, say, divers may on occasion be able to achieve something useful working off even catastrophically eroded sites. At least the existence of classical buildings beyond the present shore line may be established if nicely dressed marble blocks of the right kind are found (provided it's not the cargo of a sunken stone barge!). At Jarlshof, however, stones were used in much their natural state. There, ancient walls are to be recognised as such by their structure, not their components. Erosion of the soft matrix of the mound tumbled the old walls into the sea or onto the beach, often from a considerable height. All structure was lost, and even the missing half of the massive broch tower had simply disintegrated on being undermined and dropped over fifteen feet into the surf. A slim possibility remained however that some of the hundreds of small artefacts that must have strewn the eroded as well as the surviving parts of the site might have lodged underwater in places from which divers might recover them.

Check dives confirmed that there was no hope of tracing missing buildings, and showed that the chance of worthwhile small finds was negligible. Immediately seawards of the site, the shingle beach that lies along the base of the sea wall stops and a rugged platform of well scoured bedrock emerges. No relics of "cultural fall-out" from the erosion were identified there, and there seemed little sign of any special circumstances likely to preserve caches of artefacts in the type of high energy environment that southerly gales create along that foreshore. If anything Viking has survived at all there, it is almost certainly so rolled and battered that it would be unlikely to contribute much to archaeological knowledge.

It would undoubtedly have been nice if the remains of a line of Viking boat noosts could have been mapped underwater to define the seaward extent of the site in Rognvald's day. However, the Sumburgh team had no illusions that it would be as easy as that. Hamilton's report and stereoscopic air photographs of the area had given them an idea of what to expect and they came to Shetland prepared for real detective work here, as well as at Gulberwick.

The group who set out to reconstruct the original extent of Jarlshof was a small one, drawn from among the long-term members of the Expedition. Indeed they all fitted into Denis Mott's short-wheelbase Landrover – diving gear and all. The Sumburgh work was done towards the end, and this veteran vehicle was by then blossoming under the attentions he had been showering upon it since arriving in Shetland. Somehow, on top of keeping the electronics, hydraulics and pneumatics of the entire Expedition going (and becoming a well-known guest member of the local NAAFI), Denis contrived to swop the cylinderhead gasket, rebuild the carburettor and fettle the entire exhaust system. Eighteen hours of sunlight per day may have had something to do with it. At Jarlshof he also gave a hand with the survey measurements, as did Dave Shaw. Ian Morrison was in charge and did the underwater work with Dave.

The ranks of the divers were infiltrated by Pam Butler, refugee from the cook-house. She was only starting to learn to dive then, but could literally leave the old hands gasping with her swimming ability. There are a lot of seals around the Voe, and dark comments to Dave and Ian from Denis on shore about the dangers of cavorting with seal-women or selkie-girls drew from her the admission that she had been trained for Olympic swimming back in the States . . .

The tide was turning and visbility underwater was low as the three submerged and swam out towards the Jarlshof headland. A game of cowboys and Indians developed as they threaded their way through the great clumps of kelp jungle on the bed of the Voe. In the green murk of the sand-laden brine, dark figures lurking amid weaving fronds of tangle were difficult to spot. Just as one decided it was safe to sneak across a clear patch, the others would streak into view, snorkels hefted as six-shooters, whooping great gusts of air that shone brilliant silver in the dimness. The ambushed one would lurch picturesquely to the seabed, shot full of bubbles. Sea-horse Opera.

After two months of running the Expedition, the full-timers were all getting a bit worn, and more episodes like this would have helped rather than hindered the serious work. Certainly the projects at Jarlshof itself and those further afield in the Sumburgh area (described in the next chapter) profited from the kind of atmosphere that the less formal organisation of a smaller team can make feasible.

Two pieces of evidence were found to give grounds for setting probable maximum and minimum limits to the former extent of Jarlshof.

Firstly, although the loose sandy deposits in which the remains of the settlement are embedded were being swept away until the sea wall was built, dives disclosed nothing to suggest that the hard underlying rock platform had itself changed significantly in the single millennium since Viking times. This is not surprising. A thousand years is not long in geological terms, and there is a lot of evidence that in geologically similar areas in Scotland and Norway coastal rock platforms can retain their form for very long periods indeed in even more exposed locations than Jarlshof. Sometimes, scratch marks caused by ice, or perhaps overlays of glacial till, show that sea-shore platforms date back even before the last glaciation. It thus seems reasonable to accept that any recent changes in the solid rock of the platform have been minor at Jarlshof too. Aerial photographs suggested, and echo-sounder runs and dives confirmed, that the sea-ward edge of the platform is a quite definite one. How does this help conclusions? Since we can assume that its position has not changed much since Viking times, this well defined outer edge suggests a maximum limit for the former extent of the site, since beyond that line, lacking the defence of the high level rock foundation, soft deposits would be even more vulnerable at any relative sea level approaching that of the present day.

So far so good, but how could an estimate be made of the minimum extent of the lost land? Some notion of the absolute minimum could be got immediately by taking a plan of the site and drawing on reconstructions of the missing parts of the eroded buildings. The regular circular forms of the wheel-houses and the broch minimised guess-work in this. For example, almost exactly half the broch remains so all that need be done is to replace the missing semi-circle. And one can go beyond this. These are heavy buildings (remember the broch is a thick-walled structure, perhaps originally forty feet tall), bedded in soft deposits, well above the rock head. Originally, they could not have stood on top of a "cliff" of this soft material, or they would have collapsed it and fallen apart (as in fact happened when erosion cut in towards them). There must therefore have been at least enough of this material to seawards of them on the platform to give a situation that was stable in engineering terms. Since the archaeological evidence shows that the occupation of these structures was spread over several centuries, it seems clear that the Iron Age engineers were duly cautious in their estimates!

The broch contains a further clue that suggests that even at a minimum estimate, it was indeed originally set well back from the sea's edge. It will be recalled that the broch was a passive defence. One retreated into it, blocked up the tiny doorway and waited for the besiegers to get bored and go home. This might take some time, so it was provided with an internal well. This is now just a dry shaft, and by giving an indication of the former water table, it helps to establish a minimum estimate for the area eroded.

One thing that could invalidate this estimate would be if the old coastal water table had reflected a higher relative sea level than at present, backing up the groundwater. This seems unlikely however. There is evidence that the shore lines of Shetland have lain lower rather than higher than the present one through most recent

Diagram (not to scale) showing the well in the Broch.
1: dry as at present
2: with higher water table, implying more soft deposits to seawards over the rock platform.

millennia. Professor Gunnar Hoppe of Uppsala has shown from peat beds now submerged in Sullom Voe that six millennia ago the shore line was at least thirty feet lower than it is now. The existence elsewhere in Shetland of artificial structures, shallowly submerged and suspiciously like broch foundations, is being investigated by Ian Morrison and Owen Gander. Owen is an experienced archaeological diver who played a major part in raising the classical shipwreck being restored at Kyrenia in Cyprus. If these submerged ruins are what they seem, they will provide specific confirmation of the general probability that relative sea level was lower in Shetland at the time when brochs were being built.

If this was so, or if the local levels of land and sea were around the present level, the only way that the water table is likely to have been sufficiently high for the broch well to have been viable is for a considerable body of deposit to have existed to seawards. In other words, to have intervened between the wall and the ultimate descent of the water table towards the base level offered by sea level.

To cut a long story short, the water table evidence implies that the land available for settlement at Jarlshof did indeed formerly extend well out towards the edge of the rock platform.

Imponderables, both geological and archaeological, remain regarding the reconstruction of the Jarlshof of the period on which *Orkneyinga Saga* has focussed our attention. What precise stage had the erosion reached when Rognvald is said to have come to the Voe? Just which buildings were in use then? Were the older outhouses being used as byres for the cattle then? Indeed, did Rognvald see that particular settlement from more than a distance? Quite conceivably, the Earl may not have stepped ashore there at all. There are several other places around the Voe where boats can be beached. And the folk who laughed at him may have come from another of the settlements that there must have been around the bay. Unlike Jarlshof these have not entered the archaeological record, but such is the continuity of settlement in this area that some of the modern crofts are very likely to lie over Viking steadings.

With all these uncertainties, it would clearly be academically reprehensible to pretend that the setting of the scene in the Saga can be reconstructed precisely. Nevertheless, the work of the archaeologists and of the Expedition gives at least some idea of what it was like, and it is pleasant to indulge our imaginations and use what we know to provide a stage upon which we may envisage the end of the episode, if we assume that it was indeed at Jarlshof that Rognvald landed.

In our mind's eye, we may picture those houses we know of set much further back from the shore. Other long, low, thatched cottages may lie seawards of the broch in the area that has been lost to us. The broch itself is already ancient and dilapidated but the circumference of its foundations is still entire, for the sea bank is probably still well out towards the edge of the rock platform. Perhaps there are rough stone boat-noosts above the beach along its foot. Certainly the beach itself is busy with returning craft, and people seeing to their catches. The smoke of cooking fires is billowing out of the sooty ljoras in the thatch of the cottages, and swirling up towards the clouds. These still roll low over the headland, after the rain that had made the sea bank greasy. The Earl, white cloak grubby after his fall, and cowl askew, sets his foot more cautiously to the bank, and at the top scowls at the still chortling fishwives. Casting his rhyme over his shoulder as a parting shot, he mounts his shaggy pony and rides back northwards. A couple of prime saithe swing from a thong at his saddlebow.

Chapter 7

Reconstructing a Viking Seascape: Sumburgh at the Time of the Earls

In the last chapter, we looked rather closely at the immediate environs of Jarlshof. It is now time to step back and take a broader view of the Viking geography. Earlier, we noticed that Shetland is the nearest land across the North Sea from Norway, and that the islands lie astride sea routes leading to and from the more populous southerly part of ancient Scandinavia.

Not all Viking navigators would call in. Some certainly just used the islands as a landmark, as a set of medieval sailing directions for getting to Greenland illustrate. The navigator is instructed to set off from Hernar near Bergen and sail due west. He is told that to hold the course correctly he should pass north of Shetland so that he can just sight it in clear weather.

For many, however, the islands must have offered a convenient staging post on the seaways. For some it would be a planned stop, for others a refuge in storm. For those based in the islands themselves, the position was a good one. For instance, it offered a strategic base for mounting raids, not only down the British east coast, to such places as Lindisfarne or Jarrow, but also into the Scottish Western Isles, where Iona lies. If piracy afloat was in hand, one would not have to venture far: throughout the summer sailing season ships would come by this nodal point of routes. If legitimate trade was the aim, the position was equally advantageous. Indeed it would be surprising if Shetland did not serve as something of an entrepöt, exchanging goods from the varied hinterlands of the different seaways.

How did these run? The busiest would often be the direct link across to the Scandinavian coast, there joining routes from the Baltic, southern North Sea and indeed Arctic. Another would go out into the Atlantic, to Iceland, Greenland and perhaps even on occasion to Vinland beyond. A further route certainly went via the Western Isles and the Minch to the Isle of Man, Viking Dublin and thence southwards, eventually into the Mediterranean. Some of the North Sea traffic via the British coast may well have gone that far too.

We associate the Norsemen with the grey seas of the north, and have no difficulty in picturing them on a lava beach in Iceland, or rowing up into a fjiord with a glacier at its head. The idea of their voyaging even to parts of North America is not unfamiliar, with the recent interest in Vinland maps and sagas, and the discovery by the Ingstads of what appears to be a genuine Viking settlement, not unlike Jarlshof, at L'Anse au Meadows in Newfoundland. Somehow, however, the idea of longships nosing round sunbleached Greek headlands against a backdrop of Mediterranean blue seems less easy to reconcile with the images of our schooldays. But then, on the schoolroom walls they all had horns on their helmets too.

The pilgrimage to Palestine that Rognvald went on after his Shetland shipwreck was by no means the only visit to those waters by Norsemen. Just as Byron carved his name on the temple at Sunion, along the coast from Athens, so Norse wanderers left a Viking "Kilroy was here" in runes on a classical statue of a lion nearby in the Piraeus. This beast can now be seen in Venice. It will be remembered that according to *Orkneyinga Saga,* Eindridi, who canvassed the idea of the pilgrimage, had newly returned from Constantinople, where Vikings served regularly in the guard of the Byzantine emperors. Indeed that city, Byzantium or Constantinople

Sumburgh Head, as seen when coming from Norway

Above: *Eddie Tysick*

Left: *Don Smith of Slough S.A.C.*

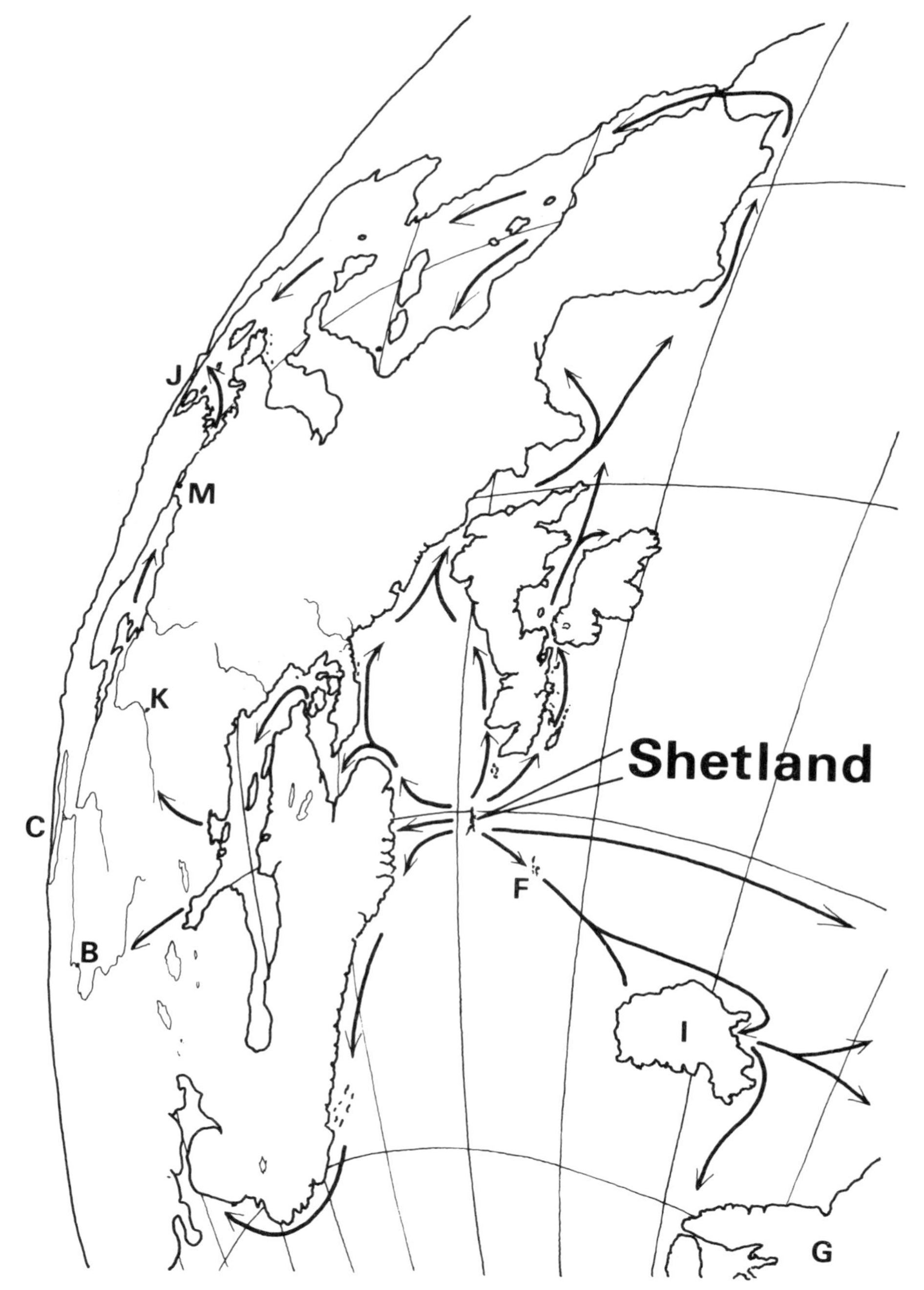

F. Faroes I. Iceland G. Greenland B. Bulghar on the Volga K. Kiev by the Dnieper C. Caspian Sea on route to Baghdad M. Miklagard (Constantinople) J. Jerusalem

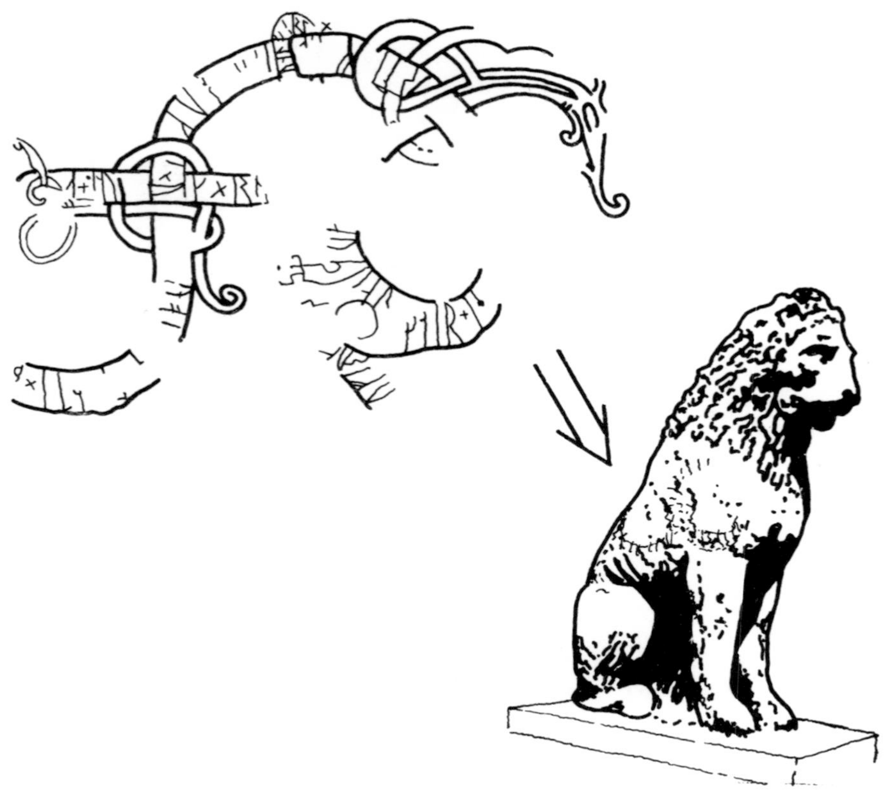

Runes on the Greek Lion

to Greeks and, later, Istambul to Turks, had its own Norse name, Miklagard.

Things like these are merely incidental symptoms of a longstanding and widespread pattern in Norse trade. Some well established routes crossed the headwaters of the Baltic rivers, and then went down the big Russian waterways. One went by Kiev on the Dnieper into the Black Sea and thence by the Bosphorus into the Mediterranean, another by Bulghar and the Volga to the Caspian and, on occasion, even to Baghdad on the Tigris. Hoards found in the Viking homelands of the north contain coins minted as far off as Bokhara, Samarkand or Tashkent, as well as in Europe.

With routes ramifying from Greenland and Iceland to Central Asia as well as Central Europe, the cargoes passing Shetland must have been diverse indeed. Timber, iron, grain, honey, salt, wax or cloth

Walrus Ivory Chessmen found in Lewis in the Outer Hebrides. The one on the left is gnawing his shield rim, in best baresark manner . . .

were useful if unexciting. We know however that from time to time the Vikings also shipped less mundane goods: walrus-hide ropes and even walrus-ivory chessmen; narwhal tusks and the occasional live polar bear; furs, feathers, falcons and possibly peacocks; amber and steatite; drinking horns, glasses and the wine to put in them; silver, spices, silk, swordblades and slaves.

How to make a rope out of a walrus . . .

The evidence for all this is widely distributed through the Viking world, but as we have seen, the remains surviving the accidents of preservation and discovery at Jarlshof reflected only the farming and fishing aspects of the Viking economy. It is dangerous to assume from this however that that was all that went on at Sumburgh. By definition, consumer goods are consumed. Some leave durable debris, others vanish. Salt and honey, furs or indeed wooden objects tend to leave few traces in the ground. Unless there is a catastrophe, and a house perhaps burns down, archaeologists are hardly likely to find valuable objects strewn in its ruins. Otherwise, these sometimes survive as grave goods. The burials of the Jarlshof folk have never been located, and anyway graves dating from after the conversion to Christianity would contain little. In any case, as suggested in the last chapter, there were almost certainly other settlements around Sumburgh that have not entered the archaeological record. Recently, for instance, work at Sumburgh airport disclosed part of a large but hitherto unsuspected prehistoric settlement.

It would be surprising indeed if Sumburgh did not have a role in long distance voyaging, even before Viking times. The sword-smith who set up at Jarlshof in the Bronze Age (and who from his style of workmanship may well himself have come from Ireland) had an output that may reflect a passing trade rather than merely local demand. Certainly, in terms of practical seafaring under sail and oar, Sumburgh occupies a key location. At this crossing point of routes, the Mainland of Shetland presents a north-south barrier well over fifty miles long. With Yell and Unst, the whole group is in fact around seventy miles overall, and the intervening straits are narrow and choked with islets. Sumburgh Head is the turning-point at the southerly end of the group. From there one can see Fair Isle, leading the way to Orkney and the Scottish mainland.

As we saw in the last chapter, the tide-race frequently presents a serious hazard to navigation off the headland. On the other hand, the various bays and inlets around it offer sheltered roadsteads and good beaching places. These have long been used not only by local fishing craft (Dr. C.A. Goodlad lists seven fishing stations there) but also by merchants. As mentioned in Chapter 2, the Pool of Virki (half a mile north of Jarlshof) was known as Dutch Pool at the start of the 17th century. It was still reported as being the best winter harbour south of Lerwick in the 18th century, but in recent years it has silted up and its role has been taken over by Grutness Voe, next door to it.

The particular interest of its geographical location, at the southern extremity of islands themselves at a crossing place of routes, suggested that it would be worth trying to evaluate Sumburgh through the eyes of seafarers at a Viking level of nautical technology. From their point of view, how did the advantages of the roadsteads and beaching places balance against the perils of the Roost? Before this could be assessed, the first necessity as at Gulberwick was to try to work out how far the coast and seabed might have changed since Viking times. Because of the area's exposure to the kind of winter seas described in the last chapter, the possibility of coastal changes by erosion is clearly also a very real one around Sumburgh in general, and not only at Jarlshof.

In this study, Ian Morrison was joined by Don Smith and his family, from London; Harry Harvey and Eddie Tysick from Tyneside; and Denis Mott of Otley. Mr. Les Isaacs, Controller at Sumburgh Airport, and the gentleman of the amphibious airport fire brigade were generous with practical help. The Shetland firemen got some amusement from the problems the assorted Sooth-Moothers had with each other's accents. The tongues of Lowland Scotland, London, Geordieland and Yorkshire were not always entirely mutually comprehensible. All those involved nevertheless found the project one of the most enjoyable parts of the whole Expedition, for reasons we shall come to in a moment.

The techniques used were broadly similar to those employed around Gulberwick. In the same way, a base map was prepared at a scale of 1:2500 (about 25" to the mile). This time the air photographs showed the distribution of sand and rock features on the seabed in the shallow areas. The details were plotted onto the base map using a photogrammetric instrument from Edinburgh University, and this saved a great deal of diving time. Instead of having to make survey measurements underwater, it was only necessary to do sample dives to check the photo interpretation.

Then, as a basis for analysing the deeper features, the paper-recording echo-sounder was again brought into play. This time, some five miles of profiling was carried out by Denis. Don acted as coxwain and despite the vagaries of the tide managed to hold course remarkably accurately with the almost keel-less inflatable boat. The egg-box like lattice of profile lines gave a vivid three-dimensional impression of the seabed, and by that stage in the Expedition the team were adept at distinguishing the even echo given by a sandy bottom from the spiky double trace indicating angular rocks with kelp jungle on top. The different types of submarine landform represented were then sampled by direct observation. The divers swam transects across them, navigating with their compasses and logging their observations as they went on their underwater notepads. Harry and Ian dug holes and used hand probes to test sand depths.

This type of diving has its satisfaction. One is engaged in detective work, and sticking the metal probe into the sand is anything but a mindless mechanical task. The sea-bed is being interrogated. Is the ridge that the echo-sounder revealed merely an ephemeral sand feature, liable to shift in the gales? Or is there only a veneer of sand over a reef of hard rock that certainly would not have changed significantly in the few centuries since Viking times? This kind of motivation has a strong grip on many scientists who dive in the line of business, and it is just as well, for often their work takes them into murk and discomfort, where the challenge of problem-solving is their only incentive for being in the water. As we shall see shortly, things were not like this at Sumburgh. The diving conditions were entrancing, in the full and original meaning of a much debased word.

What kind of results came out of the scientific work? Firstly, changes certainly have taken place since Viking times in the details of many parts of the Sumburgh coastline. In some places, superficial deposits have been eroded off or redistributed. Some major ridges constructed of heavy boulders, as well as sand features, appear to have been remodelled repeatedly. Cliff falls seem likely in several places, and Jarlshof is not the only place where soft deposits have been cut back. Another archaeological site being affected by erosion is a broch near the mouth of the Pool of Virkie. Altogether, the evidence of the power of the seas is impressive. On the other hand, it is equally clear that the basic layout of the bays at Sumburgh is largely controlled by bedrock topography, and the major features of this have certainly changed little there since the last glaciation. Areas where there is clear evidence of recent erosion of rock are very localised.

Although the basic form of the bedrock topography has remained essentially the same, sea level has not. As we saw in the last chapter, Shetland has submerged significantly in the past, and the coastline today certainly differs from that of, say, five or six thousand years ago. Some uncertainty remains about the precise sea level in Viking times. However, to invoke a change of level of sufficient magnitude to cause any radical alteration of the overall pattern of the Sumburgh coastline in the last thousand years would raise considerable difficulties.

It seems likely, then, that the basic layout of the roadsteads offered by the Bay of Quendale, the West Voe of Sumburgh and Grutness Voe is much as it was during Earl Rognvald's time. The particular lines of the sandy beaches at the heads of these bays are subject to change, but from the amount of sand present there (both

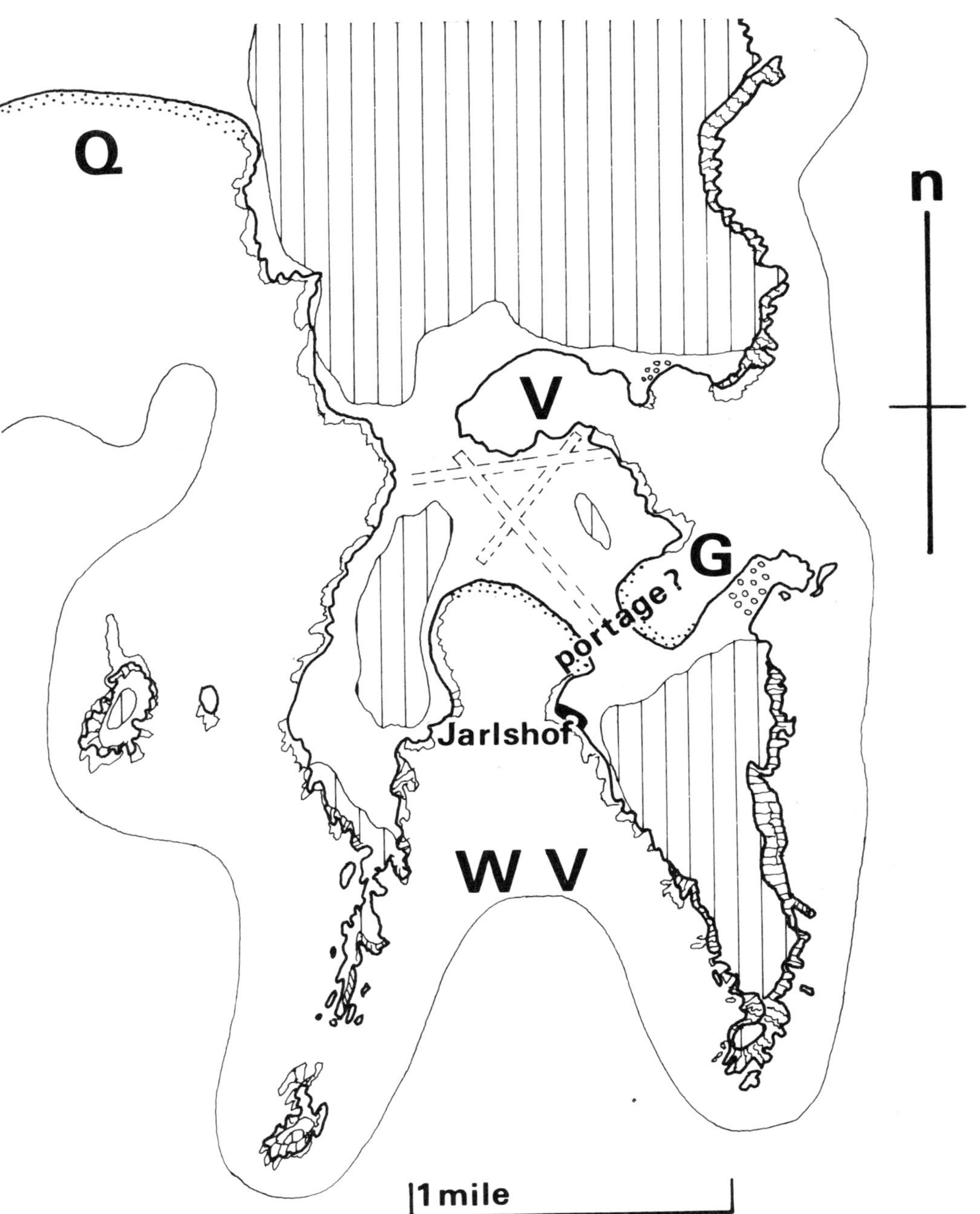

Q. Quendale Bay V. Pool of Virkie G. Grutness Voe WV. West Voe of Sumburgh. The ten fathom line is shown, and land over fifty feet above sea level is shaded. A second portage, at the head of the Pool of Virkie, seems possible but has not been marked due to doubt about the form of that bay in Viking times.

offshore and as blown sand on land) it seems likely that the Vikings also had such beaches available to them for drawing up their ships and boats.

Unlike the other bays, the Pool of Virkie has a shallow rock sill across its entrance, and, as noted, at present it is almost silted up. The silting appears to be related in part to the construction of the airfield, but it is possible that the Pool did not exist in Viking times, though the historical records tend against this.

Viewing the evidence as a whole, it would thus seem that despite its tide-race the Sumburgh area was one that offered substantial advantages to Viking seafarers. Not only was it strategically positioned in terms of long distance routes, but in local terms it offered a range of complementary roadsteads and beaching places. These between them provided shelter from weather from all points of the compass.

There is a further point. The isthmus between the West Voe and Grutness Voe is not only narrow, but low and flat. It was sandy before an airport runway was laid through it. It would not be a matter of great difficulty for Viking seamen used to the routine beaching of their light-built shallow-draught ships to run these across the isthmus, using timber rollers. Certainly it would be much less of an undertaking than the famous incident when longships were taken overland at Tarbert in Argyllshire, to symbolically sever Kintyre from the Scottish mainland.

In the Mediterranean, one often finds that in the recent past, and in antiquity too (judging from the evidence of settlement patterns and seabed finds of ancient anchors), small sailing vessels often seem to have found it judicious to put in at some convenient bay to wait for a change of wind or weather before attempting to round a dangerous promontory. It is an intriguing thought that at Sumburgh the Vikings may not have waited. Not only had they alternative shelter in the bays on either side of the peninsula, but only that short portage separated a choice of alternative east or west coast departure points for those occasions when the running of the Roost made it unwise to attempt to double Sumburgh Head by sea.

Sadly, the writer of *Orkneyinga Saga* was not interested in recording this kind of thing. As we have seen, he focussed on personalities, and incidents that could be used to depict them. Ways of doing things that would be fascinating to us in the 20th century were after all merely the commonplaces of everyday life to his contemporaries. Nevertheless, one can not but wish that we could have heard more about what Earl Rognvald saw when he visited

Sumburgh. Both the overall location and the local physiography there provide such interesting potential for seafarers and those who dealt with or preyed upon them that it is regrettable that more is not known of the area's human geography then. Jarlshof came to light by accident; the recent major find of an unsuspected ancient settlement near the airport control tower makes one wonder what is still hidden in the Links of Sumburgh and of Quendale – and how much was destroyed during the hurried wartime development of the airfield.

This book, however, is concerned not with what may or may not be underground, but rather with what the Expedition found underwater. It seems appropriate to end this last main chapter on the diving in Shetland by trying to give some impression of what it was like to experience underwater conditions there at their best. This the Sumburgh party certainly did.

By the standards of our everyday life on land, underwater it is always foggy. In some British waters, visibility of 50 *feet* (not yards) is regarded as outstanding. 15 feet is often considered good. It is worth converting this to home terms. It is equivalent to actually being pleased to be able to make out the murky outline of the door across the width of your living-room. There is a broad tendency for things to be worse in south than north Britain.

Shetland lies in a hard-rock area, well clear of the outpourings of great muddy estuaries and the cities on their banks. Visibility is by no means always good. Often plankton clouds the water, and for weeks at a time a succession of gales may keep the bottom sediments well stirred up. Falling in a protracted period of light winds and calms, the Expedition coincided with a progressive improvement of visibility offshore, as the fine suspended matter settled out. This was masked in bays like Gulberwick and the head of the Voe at Jarlshof (where the cowboys and Indians lurked) because of the routine disturbances of the sandy shallows there by the ebb and flow of the tides. The clearing was apparent off Fifa Geo, but it was below Sumburgh Head itself that its full impact was felt.

Joan Smith was boat-handler that day, and the last that the divers saw as they left the surface was her standing by in the inflatable, with a blizzard of seabirds eddying round the cliff overhead. The object of the dive was to see to what extent cliff falls had taken place since the time when the area had been scoured clear by the last glaciation. The first impression on looking down was that the echo-sounder must be wrong, the bottom seemed so close. But it was not the instrument but the divers who were wrongly calibrated. We were just not used to diving in brine that approached the clarity of drinking water, and our judgement of underwater distances was out.

It was like the Mediterranean, except that here the scene was much less barren. The long ridges of sculpted bedrock were topped with a man-high jungle of kelp, palm-like fronds sprouting with an abandon that would have delighted le Douanier. We sank past them, and swam through anastomosing alleyways paved with grey-green cobbles.

Suddenly, a seal soared past. He slipped overhead like a long silver-grey airship, then dissolved into a sleek curve. Rolling over to catch a flipperful of sea, he stopped dead and hung motionless in mid-water watching us. We edged closer, then stopped. He thought about this, then spread his flippers, and gave what can only be described as a shoulder-less shrug. This swept a double handful of brine in towards his spotted tummy, and sped him backwards over a rock ridge, out of sight.

We realised then that above us the sun had come out. Looking up, we found we were inside a dome of misty emerald and turquoise, perhaps 200 feet across. Above the kelp silhouetted in the immediate foreground, the hundred-foot radius of visibility swung upwards, until 60 or 70 feet above it intersected with the surface. This with the sun behind it appeared as a disc of some ever crinkling mirror material. As they accelerated towards it, the bubbles of our exhalations expanded into great quivering silvery saucers. One got the impression of looking down, not up, and dropping great globules of mercury towards waves in a mercury sea, at the bottom of a great bowl of blue-green glass.

Then, after the sublime came the ridiculous. Notes made, we were on our way back towards the surface when literally "out of the blue" came a rolled umbrella. Ferrule first, it sped past the divers, propelled by the alternate furling and unfurling of two smaller umbrellas at the handle end. We hope it was a cormorant, but they don't draw them like that in the bird books.

What with this apparition and his mercury notion, Ian was by then beginning to wonder whether nitrogen narcosis had somehow gripped him despite the shallow depth. He was therefore quite relieved to find on surfacing that the others too were exhilarated by what they had experienced. Don was well pleased, but Eddie was actually incoherent with delight. Harry was having to interpret to Joan what Eddie was trying to tell her about the difference between what was beneath the boat and what comes down their home Tyne in the name of water.

Sometimes in Shetland, then, it seems that vision may be as potent an element as nitrogen for producing in divers that entranced state that Captain Cousteau once named the Rapture of the Deeps.

Chapter 8

Conclusion

The story told by *Orkneyinga Saga* is a rich and highly convoluted one. Earl Rognvald had a long and adventurous career before the ambush on the bleak moors of Caithness, where a man called Stefan finally drove a spear into him. In the Saga the episode in which he and the young Earl Harald were wrecked in Shetland is not a major one, and the story of his exploit in the tide-race is an incidental anecdote. However, as suggested at the beginning of this book, in accounts of the past it is often not the major themes but rather the minor incidents that catch our imagination. We feel that we can identify more readily with them.

Certainly, by the end of the Expedition, its members felt that they had more of a gut-feeling for what the Earls and their crews had experienced than is given to most Sooth-Moothers. True, they had not been forced ashore by night in a bay near Gulberwick, like Andrew Ridland. Nevertheless, some of them had had to try to find the beach in mist or in darkness, and all were more than familiar with immersion in a North Sea brine that chilled to the bone. They had swum below the Shetland cliffs, and wondered if they could have hauled themselves clear of the surf to climb them. Several had in fact scaled the walls of Stava and Fifa Geos, while the sea-banks below the King's Knowe were at times a veritable thoroughfare for returning divers. Emerging from the chill sea, they too had been treated with great hospitality by local farmers and cottagers, sometimes in long croft-houses still reflecting the Saga-Age tradition of building laid bare at Jarlshof. Beside the ruins there, Expedition members helped to launch Viking-style yoles, and watched them fishing out by the tide-race. On their daily movements between Dunrossness and Gulberwick, they travelled through a landscape studded with Norse placenames. And they heard words that the Viking Earls would have known, used in everyday speech by the people around them.

Experiences like these, living and working with episodes from a Saga in their actual geographical setting, had their effect. Some who had come to Shetland essentially for the diving, being fully resolved to leave the bookwork to the academics, went home and spent the next winter avidly devouring all the Sagas that they could lay their hands on. Like those academics before them, they found that under the seemingly recondite and forbidding heading of "Old Norse Literature" lurks an extraordinarily vivid and varied treasure house of tales.

To others, the most important product of the Expedition was a more practical one. As mentioned in the introductory chapter, many people enjoy the process of training as divers, but then find themselves undecided as to how to apply their new skills. The experience gained on the Expedition helped in their decision making. The work in Gulberwick under the direction of Alan Bax, Nic Ashmore and Jim Gill gave them a thorough introduction to the realities of conducting a difficult search operation, and to the amount of meticulous record-keeping that archaeological operations entail. Some found that this kind of work was much less attractive than they had anticipated, and they will explore other fields in the future. Others whose interest was confirmed despite the long, arduous and at times frustrating search will provide a nucleus for future professionally-minded archaeological teams.

The academic results of the Expedition fall into several categories. On the technical side, in addition to learning more about the advantages and shortcomings of various underwater search procedures and prospecting instruments, members carried out operational trials with special survey methods. Peter Milne worked up his underwater plane tabling system, while Ian Morrison experimented with ways of integrating air photo interpretation, hydrographic survey and diving operations in geomorphological studies.

On the archaeological side, not all the activity was underwater by any means. Duncan McArdle located several previously unrecorded prehistoric sites around Gulberwick, and it will be recalled that plans were made not only of the King's Knowe but also of the exciting fortifications found on the Hevdas overlooking Stava Geo. The work in the Sumburgh area, estimating the former extent of the Jarlshof site and reconstructing what its marine setting had been like in Viking times, could be ranked either as environmental archaeology or as a study in geography. In the same way the main work of the Expedition concerning the wrecking of the Earls has aspects of archaeology, Saga scholarship, geomorphology and seamanship.

This theme of integrating diverse elements was one that recurred throughout the Expedition. Not only were its objectives interdisciplinary in the academic sense, but the variety of practical techniques and devices that had to be used in conjunction in pursuing them was little short of extraordinary. Besides the predictable paraphernalia of diving, there were days when the devices in action included a portable fire-pump, a photogrammetric plotting machine, an underwater telephone, and a submersible bolt-firing gun. The people with the skills to work them were if anything more diverse. As we have already seen, they came from many different directions in Britain and beyond. Among their number they included not merely cooks but a Butler, who was also a potter; the Expedition had its own Army, with Colonel and tank landing craft (the police force was smaller in numbers, but taller); there were ex W.R.N.S. and naval officers; students, including a musical physicist and a diving lawyer; engineers of all kinds; even a restorer of showmen's steam organs, plus a most unlikely dealer in ladies underwear, and an amphibious midwife. One could not but feel that they would do rather well if they chanced to be shipwrecked together on a desert island.

Shetland, however, is no desert island and neither was it that when the Viking Earls were wrecked there. As we have seen, the sea was then as now as much a highway as a moat for the islanders. Perhaps it was because so much of the day-to-day running of the Expedition involved thinking in practical terms about the integration of diverse concepts, techniques and personalities that the islands became so intriguing to their visitors. This type of operation is after all what the Shetlanders have been doing over the eight centuries since the days of Rognvald, producing a unique amalgam of Viking past with lively present.

The diving to be found in the waters off the islands can be amongst the most beautiful and challenging in British seas. However, even for divers, it is the islands themselves and the style of life of those who live upon them that form the chief attraction of an Expedition to Shetland.

Books and Records

Jacqueline Simpson's book on *Everyday Life in the Viking Age* (Batsford 1967 & 69; paperback, Carousel 1971) is a reliable and pleasant introduction to the Viking world. *The Viking* edited by Bertil Almgren (Tre Trikare; English edition by Watts of London 1966) is one of the most comprehensive and definitive of the large illustrated books, while the reader wishing to pursue the subject in some depth should seek the major work by Professors Peter Foote and David Wilson, *The Viking Achievement* (Sidgwick & Jackson 1970).

J.R. Nicolson's recent book *Shetland* (David & Charles, 1972) gives a far ranging and up-to-date view of the islands, while *The Northern Isles* edited by F.T. Wainwright, (1962) and the late Professor O'Dell's *Historical Geography of the Shetland Islands* (1939) are still valuable as introductions to the past of the islands. The *Excavations at Jarlshof* are reported in detail by J. Hamilton (H.M.S.O. 1956), while the history of the Scandinavian link is covered in *Scotland and Scandinavia – Studies Commemorative of the Union of Orkney and Shetland with Scotland*, a volume reprinted from the *Scottish Historical Review*, Vol. XLVIII April 1969 (Aberdeen University Press). Jakob Jakobsen's *The Dialect and Placenames of Shetland* of 1897 is a fascinating and often entertaining record of much that has been lost in this century, and can be obtained through the larger libraries. *The Shetland Folk Books* (Vols. 1-5, 1953 to '71), produced by the Shetland Folk Society, contain a delightful selection of dialect stories, poems and fiddle tunes, while *Nordern Lichts,* edited by J. Graham and T. Robertson (1964, published by the Education Committee of Shetland County Council) is an anthology of verse, prose and songs. It includes *Da Velyant Hert,* Emily Milne's poem about the cormorant, a fragment of which has been quoted, as well as a very moving tale by Tom Henderson about men lost at sea in a sixern. The song about King Orfeo which is mentioned in Chapter 2 can be heard sung by John Stickle of Shetland on *The Childe Ballads No 1,* (Topic Records 12 T 160) in the series *Folk Songs of Great Britain,* Vol 4. *Shetland Fiddle Music* from the field collections of The School of Scottish Studies of Edinburgh University is available on *Scottish Tradition 4* TN GM 117, (Tangent Records).

Books and Records

Recent works on Viking ships include Ole Crumlin-Pedersen's chapters in *Aspects of the History of Wooden Shipbuilding,* in *Maritime Monographs and Reports* of the National Maritime Museum, Greenwich (1970, No 1) and in the major *History of Seafaring based on Underwater Archaeology* edited by George Bass (Thames and Hudson, 1970), to which Arne Emil Christensen also contributes well illustrated Scandinavian material. Some of the most interesting of the easily available material on Shetland boats appears in C.A. Goodlad's *Shetland Fishing Saga* (Shetland Times Ltd. 1971) and in Edgar J. March's *Inshore Craft of Britain in the Days of Sail and Oar* (Vol. 1, 1970, David and Charles with Fishing News and International Maritime Publ. Co. of Maine, USA). Further material on Viking ships and boat building techniques appears in the *International Journal of Nautical Archaeology* (Seminar Press). This last journal carried an initial note on the Expedition in Volume 1, 1972, and Volume 2, Sept. 1973 contains *Jarlshof – The Marine environment of a Viking Settlement* by I.A. Morrison. The main academic publication of results from the Expedition thus far is the 1973 edition of the *Saga Book of the Viking Society: Earl Rognvald's Shipwreck – an investigation into saga historicity,* by Collings, Farrell and Morrison.

INDEX